General Editor JAMES SUTHERLAND
Emeritus Professor of Modern English Literature
University College London

Library of
Woodbrooke College
Selly Oak
Birmingham

POEMS OF FAITH AND DOUBT

The Victorian Age

edited by

R. L. BRETT

Professor of English, University of Hull

Edward Arnold

© R. L. BRETT 1965
First published 1965
by Edward Arnold (Publishers) Ltd.
41 Bedford Square, London WC1B 3DQ

Reprinted 1971, 1977, 1979, 1980, 1981, 1982

ISBN: 0 7131 5344 X

20023889

All Rights Reserved. No part of this publication may be reproduced, stored in a retrieval system, or transmitted in any form or by any means, electronic, mechanical, photo-copying, recording or otherwise, without the prior permission of Edward Arnold (Publishers) Ltd.

821.8

Printed and bound in Great Britain at
The Camelot Press Ltd, Southampton

General Preface

THE design of this series is to present fully annotated selections from English literature which will, it is hoped, prove satisfactory both in their breadth and their depth. To achieve this, some of the volumes have been planned so as to provide a varied selection from the poetry or prose of a limited period, which is both long enough to have developed a literary movement, and short enough to allow for adequate representation of the chief writers and of the various cross-currents within the movement. Examples of such periods are the late seventeenth century and the early eighteenth century. In other volumes the principle of selection is to present a literary kind (e.g. satirical poetry, the literary ballad). Here it is possible to cover a longer period without sacrificing the unified and comprehensive treatment which is the governing idea for the whole series. Other volumes, again, are designed to present a group of writers who form some kind of "school" (e.g. the Elizabethan sonneteers, the followers of Ben Jonson), or who were closely enough linked for their work to be brought together (e.g. the poetry of Johnson and Goldsmith).

Each volume has a full critical introduction. Headnotes, a special feature of this series, provide relevant background and critical comment for the individual poems and prose pieces. The footnotes are for the most part explanatory, giving as briefly as possible information about persons, places, allusions of one kind or another, the meaning of words, etc., which the twentieth-century reader is likely to require. Each selection aims at providing examples of the best work of the authors represented, but it is hoped that the inclusion of some less familiar pieces not available in any other collection will widen the reader's experience and enjoyment of the literature under review. The series is intended for use in universities and the upper forms of schools.

In this selection of Victorian poetry Professor R. L. Brett of the University of Hull has concentrated upon those poets who expressed most powerfully and beautifully the religious beliefs and doubts of an age which was deeply committed to intellectual enquiry and involved in rapid change. In his full and valuable introduction he draws attention to three movements of thought that were particularly significant for the Victorians: the new biblical criticism, the theories of evolution, and the growth of positivism, which denied the possibility of any knowledge about the ultimate cause of things. To the situation in which they found themselves Clough, Arnold, Tennyson, Browning and Gerard Manley Hopkins reacted in their own different ways, and all are well represented here by some of their most important work. Other poets, such as Emily Brontë, Newman, Christina Rossetti, Swinburne and Meredith, also contribute their individual bands of colour to a spectrum which ranges from confident faith, through honest doubt, to black despair. Professor Brett's selection is to be commended both for the quality of the poems chosen, and for the light that they throw on the Victorian mind in its best and most serious hours.

Acknowledgement

For permission to reprint three poems from *Poems of Gerard Manley Hopkins, ed. Robert Bridges*, second edition, the editor and publishers wish to thank the Oxford University Press.

Contents

Introduction

THE Victorian age has been accused of smugness, complacency and hypocrisy in matters of religion. These are charges which children often level against their parents. But as they grow up, children sometimes acquire greater awareness of the problems of a previous generation and an understanding of its predicaments. So, today, there are signs that we have outgrown the adolescent "smartness" of Lytton Strachey's *Eminent Victorians* and begun to realise more clearly the real qualities of the Victorian age.

Religious faith is not easily come by in any age, but in the Victorian period in particular it had to face difficulties that perhaps no other period had yet experienced to quite the same degree. From the beginning of the nineteenth century three movements of thought made onslaughts upon the stronghold of orthodoxy. These, though separable for the purpose of analysis, united in their historical effect to produce a situation in which a profound scepticism assailed everyone who tried to think honestly about religion. Firstly, there was a new approach to the authority of the Scriptures; secondly, the emergence of evolutionary theories; and thirdly, the growth of positivism, a philosophy which denied the possibility of any knowledge about the ultimate cause of things.

Few sophisticated minds at the beginning of the nineteenth century held the view that the Bible was literally true in every detail. Indeed, from the days of the early Church Fathers the Scriptures had been interpreted not only as historical narrative, but as moral and spiritual allegory. Nevertheless, the traditional attitude of believers was that the Bible was a book apart, inspired by God and the repository of that sacred truth necessary for man's salvation. The Scriptures had not yet been subjected to the historical and linguistic examination which was being applied to the classical texts of Greece and Rome. This kind of scrutiny, originated in the main by German scholars, when applied to the Scriptures made it obvious that not all the books of the Bible were of equal value as a revelation of God's will, and that the story they told was of a developing religious consciousness amongst one race, the Jews. In Britain the new Biblical criticism was accompanied by a revolution in geological studies, marked by the publication in 1830-3 of Lyell's *Principles of Geology*. Lyell's book made it very difficult to accept literally the Biblical stories of the Creation and the Flood, and thus raised the question of whether the Scriptures could be trusted as historical narrative at all.

The Biblical scholar who gave the most startling answer to this question was the German, D. F. Strauss, author of *Das Leben Jesu* (1835). Strauss's *Life of Jesus* reviews the previous attempts which had been made to write a biography of Christ and rejects them because they all start from the assumption that they are concerned with the supernatural. Strauss refuses to make this assumption and tries to account for the facts as he knew them by the ordinary canons of historical scholarship. He sees Christianity as a myth; not in the sense of an imposture deliberately invented by a group of interested partisans, but akin to Greek myth in embodying truths of great value. The groundwork of this myth had been prepared for centuries by the Messianic hopes of the Jewish people and it only needed (Strauss suggested) a figure like the human teacher, Jesus, to lead his followers to see in him a supernatural and divine Christ. Strauss was a disciple of Hegel, and Hegel's philosophy envisaged history as a self-contained and ever-developing process in which there was no place for the supernatural. Miracles, divine birth, resurrection were all ruled out, for the history of religion was really the history of man's developing thoughts about the infinite.

It was George Eliot's reading of Strauss's book, which she translated into English in 1846, and of the not dissimilar though less radical, *An Inquiry Concerning the Origin of Christianity* (1838) by her friend Charles Hennell, which first sowed the seeds of doubt in her mind. Many years later, in 1863, after reading Renan's *Life of Jesus*, George Eliot expressed, in a letter to a friend, sentiments which were beginning to be adopted by a growing number of sensitive people. "It seems to me," she wrote, "the soul of Christianity lies not at all in the facts of an individual life. . . . We can never have a satisfactory basis for the history of the man Jesus." She goes on to say that this does not invalidate the historical significance of the *idea* of Christ or what she calls "its great symbolic meanings", but for her, as for others, the basis of Christianity in historical fact has vanished. The Jesus of history has been replaced by a symbol.

What has today been called the scandal of particularity—the claim that the Incarnation is *the* central event of history and not simply *one* event in a history that goes back even before man himself started to exist—was aggravated, of course, by evolutionary theories. Darwin's *Origin of Species* appeared in 1859, but it was not the first book to advance such a theory. Before Darwin there had been Lamarck and Darwin's own grandfather, Erasmus Darwin, both of them evolutionists. Lyell's *Principles of Geology* and Chambers's *The Vestiges of Creation* (1844) had both made it difficult to uphold a belief in one divine act of Creation. Tennyson's *In Memoriam*, published in 1850, and George Eliot's essays in *The Westminster Review* in the 1850's, show in their different ways how evolutionary theories had already raised questions for Christian theology. The novelty of Darwin's work, apart from its wealth of scientific detail and observation, is indicated in the full title of his book, which is *On the Origin of Species by Means of Natural Selection, or the Preservation of Favoured Races in the Struggle for Life*. The phrase, *by Means of Natural Selection*, suggested that the evolutionary process worked by chance and not design; it seemed to remove any purpose from history and any divine providence from the universe.

Though Darwin himself regarded his book as simply concerned with biological theory, it seemed to many to bring closer to realisation the dreams and aspirations of the positivists. Auguste Comte (1798-1857), the French sociologist and founder of positivism, produced his six volumes of the *Course of Positive Philosophy* between 1830 and 1842. In this work he advanced his Law of the Three States, according to which there were three stages of human thought. At first, men had thought religiously and had interpreted nature in terms of anthropomorphic deities. This had been followed by the metaphysical stage, in which these deities had been transformed into abstract forces. The last and positive stage was one in which the true scientific explanation of nature was given. The positivists believed that they could extend their theory to embrace not only the natural but the social sciences, and could then show all human thought as subject to the same development. The natural sciences had made a dramatic breakthrough into the positive stage, but other branches of enquiry were lagging behind and giving explanations in terms of theological and metaphysical concepts. Evolutionary theory, for the positivists, promised a great step forward. It would explain not only nature but man himself, his behaviour (including his moral behaviour) and the organisation of society. By laying bare the mechanism of this evolutionary process—natural selection and the survival of the fittest—Darwin had not only confirmed Comte's thesis, but had provided the scientific evidence of the way it worked. Darwin and Comte together provided for some brave spirits the key to a new and exciting pattern of thought.

Comte was hostile to all religion, especially Christianity, but he felt that men needed a substitute for it, something to which they could submit and which would give them emotional satisfaction. For this reason he proposed the image of collective humanity as the object of men's worship, and invented an elaborate ritual and priesthood which, though secular, were modelled on those of the Roman Church. Few of his English followers accepted his proposal, and T. H. Huxley, Darwin's friend and chief disciple, dubbed Comte's religious system "Catholicism minus Christianity". Nevertheless, positivism and the religion of humanity became for many the substitute for Christianity. Such people, though agnostic, carried over into their agnosticism a stern sense of duty and a high seriousness which were almost religious in character. They felt that religious emotion was a valuable asset which could bind society together and create a veneration for the moral law. One could almost say that they worshipped God but spelled his name with a small "g" and two "o's".

Many of these agnostics were followers of John Stuart Mill, who was called by Carlyle "the Saint of Rationalism". Mill had been influenced by Comte and accepted his theory of the Three States of human development. As a young man, he had been attracted by Coleridge and had written about him sympathetically in *The Westminster Review*, but he had finally thrown Coleridge overboard in favour of Bentham and utilitarianism.[1] Mill was not a positivist in the strict sense, but as an empiricist he believed that all our knowledge and systems of morality can be derived from experience. Mill was one of the great intellectual forces of the Victorian period, but it was not only his own writings that made him so influential. His ideas were diffused throughout society by several important periodicals of the day. One of his disciples was John Morley, who left Oxford after abandoning his intention of taking holy orders. Ironically enough, he lost his faith while occupying the very rooms which had been John Wesley's at Lincoln College. It was reading Darwin after a course of John Stuart Mill, he tells us, which brought about this debâcle. Morley became editor of the *Fortnightly Review* and declared his editorial policy to be "the diffusion and encouragement of rationalistic standards in things spiritual and temporal alike". Morley is typical of many who embraced agnosticism yet looked back with regret to the days of settled faith. Writing to a friend he could exclaim, "Oh that we were in those old ages of noble, grave belief". George Meredith, who was less sympathetic to traditional faith, went so far as to say, "Cut him open and you will find a clergyman", but the same was true of many other agnostics.

Two other admirers of Mill and Darwin were George Eliot and George Henry Lewes. Lewes had preceded Morley as editor of the *Fortnightly*, and already, as editor of *The Leader*, had published papers by Huxley and Herbert Spencer which prepared the ground for the *Origin of Species*. When

[1] F. R. Leavis republished Mill's essays on Bentham and Coleridge in volume form in 1950.

Darwin's book appeared, Lewes and George Eliot welcomed it with raptures. Lewes had been sent an advance copy for a review in *Blackwood's Magazine*. He passed it on to George Eliot, who recorded her enthusiasm in her *Journal* on November 24, 1859: "A divine day. I walked out and Mrs. Congreve [the wife of a well-known positivist] joined me. Then Music, *Arabian Nights*, and Darwin."

A more militant advocate of the new thought was Leslie Stephen, who had himself been a priest of the Church of England, but who had renounced his orders. Stephen, like Morley, lost his faith through reading Darwin after being indoctrinated with the teaching of Mill and the positivists. Unlike many of his contemporaries, he cast no nostalgic look over his shoulder at the faith he had left behind. In an essay entitled *Are We Christians?*, which first appeared in *Fraser's Magazine* and was later published in *Essays on Freethinking and Plainspeaking* (1873), he wrote: "Let us shake the dust off our feet, and taking reason for our guide, and Mr. Darwin for the best modern expounder of the Universe, go boldly forward to whatever may be in store for us." Stephen had little sympathy for those Christians who tried to reconcile the new way of thinking with their religious belief. He was impatient with the liberal-minded, including Broad Church theologians like Jowett, the Master of Balliol, or poets like Matthew Arnold, who tried to accommodate their belief to the advance of knowledge. In an essay, *Religion as a Fine Art*, he charged both parties with intellectual dishonesty; with trying to eat their Christianity and still have it:

> Whether you evade the conflict between science and theology by saying that the ancient dogmas are to be accepted without any reference to reason, or to be accepted because they may be twisted into any meaning whatever, or to be accepted simply because you can get up a sham belief in them if you try very hard, you are equally approximating to the same principle that they belong to the sphere of poetry instead of history.

One can accept the Gospels as a beautiful myth, if one wishes, says Stephen in effect, but this is not the traditional teaching of the Church. Nor will a myth live if it is not rooted in fact. Poets may use the traditional dogmas of Christianity, declares Stephen, but in the end these dogmas will die as surely as the gods and goddesses of the classical world have died.

> The gods of the Pagan pantheon led a kind of posthumous existence in poetry, long after they had died out of the living faith of the world; but they suffered from a slow but inevitable decay, which made them too shadowy, by degrees, even for poetical use.

But Stephen was equally scornful of those who held to traditional orthodoxy and made no attempt to reconcile their faith with new discoveries. He had nothing but contempt for the revival of interest in the church of the Fathers and in medievalism. With heavy irony he wrote of the Tractarians, "clergymen who succeed in accomplishing very fairly the surprising feat of living in two centuries at once," and of poets (presumably Tennyson and the Pre-Raphaelites in particular) who "affect an infantile lisp, and tell us legends of old times as naturally as if human beings at the present day had still a lively interest in them." The modern version of the ancient church, he concludes with a touch almost worthy of Swift, "resembles its original as minutely as the Chinese imitation of a steam engine —the only fault of which is that it won't work."

How fair was Stephen to those who clung to their beliefs? Not everyone in the nineteenth century lost his faith as did those we have been considering. If John Stuart Mill's philosophy was the great force making for scepticism and positivism, ranged against it was the thought of Coleridge, that other great seminal figure of the century whom Mill had admired but rejected, even if regretfully.

As a young man Coleridge had visited Germany in company with Wordsworth in 1798, when the first edition of *Lyrical Ballads* was in the press. He had stayed there for almost a year at the University of Göttingen. During this time he had learned the German language, studied German philosophy, and made himself acquainted with the beginnings of the higher criticism in biblical studies. From this time onwards Coleridge kept in touch with German thought, with the result that he was one of the first and ablest minds in the nineteenth century to give theology a deeper philosophical basis. As Mill recognised in his essay on Coleridge, the situation which faced his contemporaries forced on them either one of two solutions to the problem of faith. Either with Bentham they could reject faith altogether or with Coleridge they could attempt to give it a more philosophical *rationale*.

Coleridge's theory of the imagination has an importance which is not confined to literature. He describes the imagination in *Biographia Literaria* as "the agent of the reason", and he identifies the imagination with the reason in the sense that the reason in certain aspects operates by means of the imagination. There are truths, and those of the highest kind, he maintains, which can be expressed and apprehended only in imaginative terms. "An IDEA in the highest sense of the word," he writes in Chapter IX of *Biographia Literaria*, "cannot be conveyed but by a symbol." He sees the imagination as the medium through which the artist expresses truths which are the concern not only of the pure intellect but the entire personality. "The poet, described in ideal perfection," he declares, "brings the whole soul of man into activity, with the subordination of its faculties to each other according to their relative worth and dignity. He diffuses a tone and spirit of unity that blends, and (as it were) *fuses*, each into each, by that synthetic and magical power, to which I would exclusively appropriate the name of Imagination" (Ch. XIV). One of Coleridge's main endeavours was to extend the scope of the term *reason*, to free it from the narrow confines of eighteenth-century philosophy which restricted it to no more than the power of *reasoning*, and restore to it the Platonic conception which saw it as the whole soul of man, embracing intellect, understanding, imagination, feelings and the will. In this enlarged sense man's reason will operate not only through logical argument, but by myth and symbol and in the commitment of the will in response to the apprehension of the truth.

We can see how this doctrine of the imagination influenced Coleridge's approach to the Bible. In *The Statesman's Manual* (the subtitle of which was *The Bible the Best Guide to Political Skill and Foresight: A Lay Sermon*), published in 1816, he declared that "It is among the miseries of the present age that it recognises no medium between literal and metaphorical". He rejects the historical and political writings of the century that had gone before as bedevilled by its mechanistic philosophy. They are, he contends, "the product of an unenlivened generalising understanding", not the works of imagination. The figures and events of the Scriptures, on the other hand, are "the living educts [i.e. representations] of the imagination". Coleridge did not mean by this that the Bible is fiction, nor on the other hand, did he think the only alternative to this a theory of plenary inspiration which held that every item in it is literally and historically true. He viewed the Bible as both myth and history. It reveals the truth about God himself and about man's nature and destiny

> . . . in images of the senses, and . . . gives birth to a system of symbols, harmonious in themselves, and consubstantial with the truths of which they are the conductors. . . . The truths and the symbols that represent them move in conjunction and form the living chariot that bears up (for us) the throne of the Divine Humanity. Hence, by a derivative, indeed, but not a divided influence, and though in a secondary yet in more than a metaphorical sense, the Sacred Book is worthily entitled the Word of God. . . . In the Scriptures therefore both facts and persons must of necessity have a twofold significance, a past and a future, a temporary and a perpetual, a particular and a universal application. They must be at once portraits and ideals.

In *Confessions of an Inquiring Spirit*, which was published in 1840, six years after his death, Coleridge elaborated his views in a remarkably prophetic way, to prepare those who were left to withstand the onslaught on Christianity that he realised must come. He outflanked the attacks against the Bible of critics like Strauss by asserting that the Bible carried the evidence of its own truth. "The Bible and Christianity," he declared, "are their own sufficient evidence." By this he meant that the Bible when properly read will speak to man's condition, will answer man's deepest needs, and match the truth that God has revealed in man's own spirit. But finally its truth can only be confirmed by commitment. In the concluding chapter of *Biographia Literaria* he expresses his conviction that the rationality of Christianity cannot be demonstrated by logic but is vindicated by right reason, that is, by the appeal it makes when lived out in practice.

> "In order to [achieve] an efficient belief in Christianity," he writes, "a man must have been a Christian, and this is the seeming *argumentum in circulo*, incident to all spiritual truths . . . as long as we attempt to master by the reflex acts of the Understanding what we can only *know* by the act of *becoming. Do the will of my Father, and ye shall know whether I am of God.*"

Coleridge's thought influenced a wide variety of people and movements, and all the more so because he belonged to no school or party himself. Most directly he inspired the Rev. F. D. Maurice and his many followers. Maurice was the founder of Christian socialism, a profound thinker whose liberal theology brought about his expulsion from a professorship at King's College, London in 1853; an incident which occasioned Tennyson's lines:

> Should eighty-thousand college-councils
> Thunder "Anathema", friend, at you;
> Should all our churchmen foam in spite
> At you, so careful of the right,
> Yet one lay-hearth would give you welcome
> (Take it and come) to the Isle of Wight.

But the Anglo-Catholics as well as the liberals were indebted to Coleridge. Though Newman had formed his theological opinions before he came to read Coleridge, he recognised when he did so the similarity of their beliefs. The Tractarians went beyond Coleridge in insisting that the message of the Bible must be supported by the authority of an apostolic or (for Newman and those who went with him into the Church of Rome) an infallible church. But they endorsed his rejection of the narrow intellectualism of the eighteenth century, and it is true to say that the Oxford Movement was in many ways a child of the Romantic Revival.

At the other end of the theological spectrum were those like Carlyle, who, though he thought orthodox Christianity would die, believed that ultimate reality was apprehensible only by intuition and symbol and not by science, or those like Matthew Arnold, who was impatient of all creeds and dogmas and believed that God

> Hath look'd on no religion scornfully
> That men did ever find.

For Arnold, the imagination took the place of reason. Unlike Comte, who thought that the last phase in man's development would replace religion by science and positivism, he considered that religion would be supplanted by poetry, that the poet would take over the function of the priest "to interpret human life afresh and to supply a new spiritual basis to it".

What made Matthew Arnold's teaching so attractive to his contemporaries was the possibility it offered of a religion without dogma. As might have been expected, this kind of religion was often vague and confused. Arnold defined God in *Literature and Dogma* (1873) as "the eternal not ourselves which makes for righteousness", which led the philosopher, F. H. Bradley, to declare that this was no more profound than saying that "the habit of washing . . . might be termed 'the Eternal not ourselves that makes for cleanliness'". Arnold, in like manner, declared that "The true meaning of religion is thus not simply morality, but morality touched by emotion". Such a declaration, though it might not stand up to rigorous scrutiny, chimed in with a growing consciousness that the positivists' creed offered little in the way, not only of spiritual, but even of emotional sustenance. The realisation that the operation of the sceptical intellect may atrophy the power of the imagination and dry up the springs of feeling was present to the best minds of the period. Disinfectant may be all very well and a useful commodity, but it does not provide a staple diet. Morley was one of those who began to feel, as the century wore on, that the attempt to account for human behaviour in scientific terms alone would not do. "Positivism," he wrote, "has no book of martrys and high examples. Above all it does not strike the imagination." Darwin's *Autobiography*, too, is a sad record of the price he paid for his scientific achievement. First, he tells us, he lost his love of music, then his sense of wonder, then his consciousness of God. "My mind," he confesses, "seems to have become a kind of machine for grinding general laws out of large collections of facts."

Indeed, as time passed, the high hopes and aspirations of the unbelievers and agnostics began to give way to a deepening scepticism about the foundations on which they had planned to build a new system of thought. They had substituted for Christianity a religion of morality, and evolution had suggested that mankind would evolve towards ever higher patterns of behaviour. Leslie Stephen's *Science of Ethics* (1882) was only one of many endeavours to base morality upon evolution. Moral development was seen by him as part of the evolutionary mechanism by which mankind would survive. The survival of the fittest implied for him the survival of the morally fittest. But this is an assumption for which Darwin's theory gives no support. When Darwin speaks of the survival of the fittest all he means is that those who survive are fittest to survive. This is a tautology which leaves no room for moral categories. It is impossible to conjure "ought" out of "is".

The realisation of this truth began to dawn on even the most enthusiastic of the evolutionists. T. H. Huxley, nicknamed "Darwin's bulldog" because of his ardent support of evolutionary theory, had to admit at the end of his life, when he gave the Romanes Lectures at Oxford on *Evolution and Ethics* (1893), that morality is not acting in accordance with Nature, but acting against Nature. "Social progress means," he said, "a checking of the cosmic process at every step." It means not the survival of the fittest, but the survival of those "who are ethically best". Mill himself left *Three Essays on Religion*, published posthumously in 1874, which, to the consternation of some of his followers, came close to a belief in theism. In the last of these essays he suggests that the "adaptations" in Nature described by Darwin "afford a large balance of probability in favour of creation by intelligence", but in the first essay he finds Nature indifferent to morality. Indeed, Nature in its "perfect and absolute recklessness" could be called immoral. "Nearly all the things which men are hanged or imprisoned for doing to one another, are nature's every day performances."

The pattern of Victorian thought we have traced can be seen in the poetry of the period, and indeed its poets are perhaps the best interpreters of the age. This is truer of some of the poets and poems in this selection than of others. John Keble, for instance, at his best, and it was a best only fitfully achieved, represents an Anglican piety allied to a poetic purity that takes one back to Herbert and the seventeenth century. Christina Rossetti's poetry expresses a mystical faith which is personal rather than representative of her age. Dante Gabriel Rossetti's attitude towards Christianity, although reverential, was almost entirely an aesthetic one. In this he is akin to Lionel Johnson. But while Johnson's Catholicism can be seen as typical of a certain Victorian mood in its retreat from religious questioning to an escapist vision of the past, and as a version of Arnold's substitution of art for religion, Rossetti's poetic expression is highly individual, a product of his own temperament as much as of external forces.

These poets, perhaps, are as much individual as representative. But the rest of the poets chosen for this selection all illustrate the religious temper of their time, its faith, its doubts and conflicts. And they do so in a series of contrasts. Emily Brontë's *No coward soul is mine*, for instance, is an affirmation of faith in the immortality of the soul based upon a belief in a personal God. George Eliot's *O may I join the choir invisible* looks only for an immortality in the lives of future generations, who may be inspired by the virtue and courage of the present. Newman's *Lead Kindly Light* is a prayer for Christian obedience, which is in sharp contrast to the fierce rebelliousness of Swinburne. The religion of humanity, like other religions, can be preached with either humility or *hubris*. Many Victorian unbelievers walked humbly with their non-existent God, but not Swinburne. To us, today, who have witnessed man's inhumanity to man on a larger scale than perhaps any previous generation, his exultant cry of "Glory to Man in the highest! for Man is the master of things", must seem not so much blasphemous as cruelly ridiculous.

George Meredith is altogether a better poet than Swinburne. Meredith, like all sensitive men, was perplexed by the finitude and transience of human life and especially by the pain and suffering in the natural order. The only consolation he could find was the hope that these are parts of an immanent process that will eventually transcend them. Men must bear their lot with the consciousness that they are serving a process which they cannot see completed. The individual fulfils himself by recognising his unity with Nature and not by rebelling against it. To many this will seem cold comfort, and it suggests an optimistic view of Nature that merits in some degree Mr. E. M. Forster's jibe about "the home counties masquerading as the universe" in Meredith's poetry. Certainly it does little to help us accept the kind of happening—the death by drowning of five Franciscan nuns—which inspired Gerard Manley Hopkins to write *The Wreck of the Deutschland.* How can one reconcile the horrible and apparently senseless death of five innocent individuals with a belief in God as a loving Father? The answer which Hopkins's faith provides, lies not in subordinating the individual to the universe, but in the recognition that it is a terrible thing to fall into the hands of the living God, for this may demand sacrifice and even death. Moreover, the poem illuminates his conviction that God's wrath is at one with his mercy; and that even in our destruction we are safe in God's providence. It was a belief reached not by intellectual means only, but wrung from him by great spiritual and emotional anguish, as the "terrible sonnets" likewise show.

Even Arnold and Clough, though they have so much in common, reveal in their poetry a contrast of religious attitudes. Both were acutely aware of the difficulties that beset religious faith and also of the loss to society and the individual which would be brought about by jettisoning it. The key-note of their poetry is regret and sadness, and in both there is a resolve to bear stoically the burden of uncertainty. But "immortal longings" keep breaking in, as Arnold acknowledged in *The Buried Life*:

> But often, in the world's most crowded streets,
> But often, in the din of strife,
> There rises an unspeakable desire
> After the knowledge of our buried life.

At times like these man is given a glimpse of the answer to his quest,

> And then he thinks he knows
> The hills where his life rose,
> And the sea where it goes.

But are such moments of vision trustworthy? Arnold only "thinks he knows"; Wordsworth would have *known*. Clough would have said, "does not know". Arnold's poetry was all written when he was a young man, and he left it behind to pursue his tasks as an educationist and as a critic of society and literature. For him, life demanded a practical answer; this was the only way of breaking out of the paralysis of doubt. For Clough there is no answer to the loss of belief except a determination to live according to the best he can perceive, and the faint hope, expressed in *Through A Glass Darkly*, that

> . . . when we
> That ampler life together see,
> Some true result will yet appear
> Of what we are, together, here.

James Thomson, the author of *The City of Dreadful Night*, and Lionel Johnson provide the interesting spectacle of two men who take up positions of extreme opposition in religious matters and yet have much in common. Thomson was an avowed atheist and Johnson a Roman Catholic who exhibited all the zeal of a convert; and yet the personalities of the two men were remarkably alike. Both of them had immature and neurotic characters, both sought relief from depression and insomnia in drink, and both died in degrading circumstances at a comparatively early age, because of alcoholism. Moreover, for all their differences in religious opinion, there is much that unites them as poets. Poetry, for both of them, was an expression of a highly charged emotionalism. Thomson's writing is characterised by self-pity and Johnson's by an aestheticism that makes his art more important than the religion it seeks to serve. One does not wish to sit in judgment, or minimise the immense suffering their personalities brought upon them, but, nevertheless, it remains true that neither reached the greatest heights or depths of religious poetry. Their belief, or unbelief (and unbelief is really another form of belief), became for them an escape from reality rather than a search for truth, and this had its effect upon their writing.

When we come to the two major poets of the period, Tennyson and Browning, we still find contrast, but a contrast that reveals them as complementary to each other. And the manner of this is paradoxical; for Tennyson, who was a Christian, demonstrates in his poetry that religious faith must always be accompanied by doubt, while Browning, who was not an orthodox Christian, maintains that doubt itself necessitates faith.

T. S. Eliot has written of how *In Memoriam* was welcomed by the Victorians as a message of hope and faith, whereas its real theme is tragic and doubting. "It is not religious because of the quality of its faith," but "because of the quality of its doubt", writes Eliot. "Its faith is but a poor thing, but its doubt is a very intense experience." One may not, perhaps, take such a harsh view of Tennyson's faith as Eliot, but on the main issue he is right. *In Memoriam* was written before Darwin's *Origin of Species* appeared, but already Tennyson was well informed about the new geological discoveries and evolutionary theories. From the first he was enthusiastic about the vistas of thought these opened up; they suggested a divine purpose in the universe and the perfectibility of human nature. Evolution showed the way in which man could progress from ape to angel. In *Locksley Hall*, which was written as early as the 1830's, he had expressed his confident belief:

> Yet I doubt not thro' the ages one increasing purpose runs,
> And the thoughts of men are widen'd with the process of the suns,

and had welcomed the prospect of the future:

> Not in vain the distance beacons. Forward, forward let us range,
> Let the great world spin for ever down the ringing grooves of change.

In Memoriam expresses something of the same confidence. It is written as a vindication of faith in the midst of despair, and the vindication depends in part upon a *rapprochement* between theology and the new science. Man is "the herald of a higher race" and Tennyson sees "the one far-off divine event to which the whole creation moves", not as the Incarnation or Crucifixion, but as the summit of the evolutionary movement. Evolution is not the descent of man, but the ascent. And yet in reading *In Memoriam* one is conscious of other forces; forces linked with Tennyson's own personality and his less conscious thoughts—his insecurity, his fear of death and physical dissolution, his sense of loneliness in an indifferent universe. Carlyle was clever enough to see this side of Tennyson, and, when writing to Emerson, he remarked that Tennyson carried about inside him "a bit of chaos".

These two things, the cosmic vision and the nightmare of chaos, form the co-ordinates of Tennyson's poetic sensibility. But the nightmare is perhaps the more characteristic element of his genius. Nothing brings out more clearly this dualism in Tennyson and in the entire Victorian age than a comparison of the two *Locksley Hall* poems. In the earlier poem the youthful hero looked to the future with hope and aspiration. European culture had achieved the highest expression, as yet, of human endeavour, but this was only a prelude. In *Locksley Hall, Sixty Years After* (1886), written when Tennyson himself was aged seventy-seven, the same hero is an old man of eighty. He looks back on his youthful confidence but finds little now to justify it. Man, as always, seems to be at the cross-roads; one way lies chaos, the other the promise of cosmos, order and unity.

> Chaos, Cosmos! Cosmos, Chaos! who can tell how all will end?
> Read the wide world's annals, you, and take their wisdom for your friend.

But history, as the nineteenth century wore on, had hardly seemed to justify political optimism either nationally or internationally.

> Chaos, Cosmos! Cosmos, Chaos! once again the sickening game;
> Freedom, free to slay herself, and dying while they shout her name.

Gladstone, the great Liberal statesman, took Tennyson to task for expressing reactionary opinions when he reviewed the poem in *The Nineteenth Century*, but Tennyson was surely right in thinking that a *laissez-faire* and optimistic belief in automatic progress could be a delusion. Tennyson does not dispute the need for progress, but, he insists, it is often hardly achieved:

> Forward then, but still remember how the course of Time will swerve,
> Crook and turn upon itself in many a backward streaming curve.

Tennyson does not deny the truth of evolution, but it is not an escalator which will carry mankind upwards without effort. He refers to the popular catchword 'Evolution' with trenchant irony:

> Is there evil but on earth? or pain in every peopled sphere?
> Well be grateful for the sounding watchword 'Evolution' here,
> Evolution ever climbing after some ideal good,
> And Reversion ever dragging Evolution in the mud.

The brave optimism which looked forward to a time of universal peace may be proved just a wish-fulfilment dream:

> Earth at last a warless world, a single race, a single tongue— . . .
> Warless? when her tens are thousands, and her thousands millions, then—
> All her harvest all too narrow—who can fancy warless men?
> Warless? war will die out late then. Will it ever? late or soon?
> Can it, till this outworn earth be dead as yon dead world the moon?

Man is what he always was, half an ape and half an angel. Nature cannot solve man's problems.

For Browning, too, though he had a sensitive appreciation of natural beauty, spiritual and moral values are realised only in men and women. Even here they are realised only partially, since man is always conscious of a good which constantly eludes him, of a perfection for which he strives but never attains. This suggests that man cannot be explained entirely in naturalistic terms, but belongs to a supernatural order:

> Ah, but a man's reach should exceed his grasp,
> Or what's a heaven for?

Browning was a man of wide sympathies, both personally and intellectually. We know that he admired Mill, and yet, at the same time, one of the greatest influences on his life and work was Carlyle's notion that human experience symbolises a spiritual world which makes a demand upon the individual. Browning's mother brought him up in an atmosphere of cheerful but pious non-conformist Christianity. While he never considered himself an orthodox Christian, he was a theist with a sympathetic understanding of the Christian tradition and of the Bible. What he retained of his mother's teaching was above all, perhaps, the evangelical emphasis that religion is concerned with the response of the individual to God. In *Christmas Eve* it is not only the theology of the Mount Zion Chapel which seizes his attention, but the odd assortment of persons who make up the congregation:

the fat, weary woman,
Panting and bewildered, down-clapping
Her umbrella with a mighty report

and

the many tattered
Little old-faced, peaking, sister-turned-mother
Of the sickly babe she tried to smother
Somehow up, with its spotted face.

Most of Browning's poems dealing with religion are in the form of dramatic monologues, and some modern critics have seen this as an attempt on his part to dodge the religious issue, to hide behind the *persona* of a dramatic character. Even his wife thought that he should abandon dramatic techniques and speak in his own voice. But quite apart from his poetic genius, which seemed best suited to this form, we can see that his beliefs were best expressed dramatically. For Browning believed that faith is the commitment of the individual, and his dramatic monologues present characters—often in a moment of crisis—who reveal to us the nature of such commitment, or their inability to make it. Nowhere is Browning's insistence on the need for one to commit oneself, to act (even without full knowledge of the consequences), put more vividly than at the end of *The Statue and the Bust*. Two lovers, centuries ago in Florence, failed to run away together, not because of moral scruples (though their love was illicit) but through failure of nerve, convention, and then sheer apathy. For Browning their inaction was a greater sin than the action they contemplated but failed to achieve.

The counter our lovers staked was lost
As surely as if it were lawful coin:
And the sin I impute to each frustrate ghost
Is, the unlit lamp and the ungirt loin,
Though the end in sight was a vice, I say.
You of the virtue, (we issue join)
How strive you? *De te, fabula!*

At the heart of religious experience lies the question of to what or to whom we commit ourselves. One answer is that ultimate reality must be in some sense personal. The highest we can see and do is found in human nature, so that the *summum bonum* must be like the best in ourselves, but at a far higher level. This theme is developed by Browning in *Saul*. David has found the king sunk in deep depression, he does his best to comfort him but cannot rouse him from his apathy. He is delivered from despair at the ineffectiveness of his love for the king by a vision in which he perceives that the love of God must be like his love, but infinitely more so, and, because perfect, all-powerful, and that this love will be manifested in the Messiah.

But can we trust such a vision? How do we know it is true? In *An Epistle of Karshish* Browning relates the story of an Arab physician of the first century who encounters Lazarus and is confronted with the preposterous story that this man had been raised from the dead. The story fascinates Karshish, but can he believe it? Suppose that "the All-Great were the all-loving too". The poem illustrates Browning's conviction that science cannot explain the mystery of human existence, and raises the question of what other foundations are possible for belief. *A Death in the Desert* (described by Archbishop William Temple as the best commentary on St. John's Gospel) is an imaginary account of the death of St. John, the evangelist. As he lies dying, John realises that the time is approaching when no one will be left who actually met and knew Jesus. Future generations, doubting the authenticity of John's record of Christ's life and death, may well feel that Divine Love cannot be proved by the testimony of the human heart alone, and may argue that men see in Christ only what they find best in themselves. But, says John, those who treat Christ as an anthropomorphic invention are spiritually blind. To find love in ourselves and yet deny it to ultimate reality is a form of spiritual arrogance which tempts man to usurp the place of God. Man must walk humbly, admitting his own weakness and ignorance, as well as his own potential goodness, and then he will be led to recognise that

> the acknowledgment of God in Christ
> Accepted by the reason, solves for thee
> All questions in the earth and out of it.

The Gospel, as Coleridge had maintained, is the best explanation of man's own nature. Bishop Blougram is no St. John, but his *Apology* is a corollary to *A Death in the Desert.* Doubt, he contends, is just as difficult to sustain as faith. In fact, it is only another kind of faith, and a faith which proves very unsatisfactory for the business of living. Faith is the leap in the dark that all men must make, but let us be sure we leap in the right direction.

It is unfashionable in some quarters, today, to expect poets to have a philosophy, and no one requires the poet to be either a priest or a prophet. But is there not an opposite danger; that we may confine poetry to the trivial and make it peripheral to the real issues of human existence? The questions that faced the Victorians are still with us, and when we read their poetry with unprejudiced minds it is suprising how fresh and vital it remains. It may be that they wrote too much poetry, or that too much of it was an escape from reality into a world of make-believe. But then, they had no cinema or television. When the large bulk of Victorian poetry has been sifted there remains a great deal that deserves to rank with the best of other ages. There is a great deal, too, that anticipates both in form and content the poetry of our own century. To read it may help us to understand more fully not only the Victorians but ourselves.

Emily Brontë

NO COWARD SOUL IS MINE

CHARLOTTE BRONTË tells us that this was the last poem her sister wrote. It was composed in January 1846, nearly three years before the author's death. In some of Emily Brontë's poems there is a pagan identification of the soul with Nature similar to that in Meredith's poetry and matching the mood of *Wuthering Heights*. In this and other poems, however, she expresses a belief in immortality beyond the natural order.

No coward soul is mine,
No trembler in the world's storm-troubled sphere:
I see Heaven's glories shine,
And Faith shines equal, arming me from Fear.

5 O God within my breast,
Almighty, ever-present Deity!
Life, that in me has rest,
As I, undying Life, have power in Thee!

Vain are the thousand creeds
10 That move men's hearts: unutterably vain;
Worthless as withered weeds,
Or idlest froth amid the boundless main,

To waken doubt in one
Holding so fast by Thy infinity,
15 So surely anchored on
The steadfast rock of Immortality.

With wide-embracing love
Thy Spirit animates eternal years,
Pervades and broods above,
20 Changes, sustains, dissolves, creates, and rears.

Though earth and moon were gone,
And suns and universes ceased to be,
And Thou wert left alone,
Every existence would exist in Thee.

25 There is not room for Death,
Nor atom that his might could render void:
Thou—THOU art Being and Breath,
And what THOU art may never be destroyed.

John Keble

THE following two poems are taken from Keble's *The Christian Year*, first published in 1827. *The Christian Year* became a favourite manual of devotion with those who were influenced by the Oxford Movement in the Church of England. The book follows the liturgy of the Church's year as set out in the Book of Common Prayer. Keble's poetry captures something of the serene and quiet piety of seventeenth-century Anglican poetry, especially that of Herbert. The first poem is written as a hymn for Evening Prayer; the second is for reading on the Tuesday before Easter.

EVENING HYMN

Abide with us: for it is toward evening, and the day is far spent. *Luke*, xxiv, 29.

'Tis gone, that bright and orbèd blaze,
Fast fading from our wistful gaze;
Yon mantling cloud has hid from sight
The last faint pulse of quivering light.

5 In darkness and in weariness
The traveller on his way must press,
No gleam to watch on tree or tower,
Whiling away the lonesome hour.

Sun of my soul! Thou Saviour dear,
10 It is not night if Thou be near:

Oh! may no earth-born cloud arise
To hide Thee from Thy servant's eyes.

When round Thy wondrous works below
My searching rapturous glance I throw,
15 Tracing out Wisdom, Power, and Love,
In earth or sky, in stream or grove;—

Or by the light Thy words disclose
Watch Time's full river as it flows,
Scanning Thy gracious Providence,
20 Where not too deep for mortal sense:—

When with dear friends sweet talk I hold,
And all the flowers of life unfold;
Let not my heart within me burn,
Except in all I Thee discern.

25 When the soft dews of kindly sleep
My wearied eyelids gently steep,
Be my last thought, how sweet to rest
For ever on my Saviour's breast.

Abide with me from morn till eve,
30 For without Thee I cannot live:
Abide with me when night is nigh,
For without Thee I dare not die.

Thou Framer of the light and dark,
Steer through the tempest Thine own ark:
35 Amid the howling wintry sea
We are in port if we have Thee.

The Rulers of this Christian land,
'Twixt Thee and us ordained to stand,—
Guide Thou their course, O Lord, aright,
40 Let all do all as in Thy sight.

Oh! by Thine own sad burthen, borne
So meekly up the hill of scorn,
Teach Thou Thy Priests their daily cross
To bear as Thine, nor count it loss!

45 If some poor wandering child of Thine
Have spurned, to-day, the voice divine,
Now, Lord, the gracious work begin;
Let him no more lie down in sin.

Watch by the sick: enrich the poor
50 With blessings from Thy boundless store:
Be every mourner's sleep to-night
Like infants' slumbers, pure and light.

Come near and bless us when we wake,
Ere through the world our way we take;
55 Till in the ocean of Thy love
We lose ourselves in Heaven above.

FILL HIGH THE BOWL

They gave Him to drink wine mingled with myrrh: but he received it not. *Mark*, xv, 23.

"Fill high the bowl, and spice it well, and pour
The dews oblivious: for the Cross is sharp,
The Cross is sharp, and He
Is tenderer than a lamb.

5 "He wept by Lazarus' grave—how will He bear
This bed of anguish? and His pale weak form
Is worn with many a watch
Of sorrow and unrest.

2 *oblivious:* i.e. that will bring oblivion. The wine and myrrh were offered as an opiate to dull the pain of the crucifixion.

5 *Lazarus:* brother of Martha and Mary, was raised from the dead by Jesus. St. John (xi, 35) records that Jesus wept over the dead Lazarus.

"His sweat last night was as great drops of blood,
10 And the sad burthen pressed Him so to earth,
The very torturers paused
To help Him on His way.

"Fill high the bowl, benumb His aching sense
With medicined sleep."—O awful in Thy woe!
15 The parching thirst of death
Is on Thee, and Thou triest

The slumbrous potion bland, and wilt not drink:
Not sullen, nor in scorn, like haughty man
With suicidal hand
20 Putting his solace by:

But as at first Thine all-pervading look
Saw from Thy Father's bosom to the abyss,
Measuring in calm presage,
The infinite descent;

25 So to the end, though now of mortal pangs
Made heir, and emptied of Thy glory a while,
With unaverted eye
Thou meetest all the storm.

Thou wilt feel all, that Thou mayst pity all;
30 And rather wouldst Thou wrestle with strong pain,
Than overcloud Thy soul,
So clear in agony,

Or lose one glimpse of Heaven before the time.
O most entire and perfect sacrifice,
35 Renewed in every pulse
That on the tedious Cross

Told the long hours of death, as, one by one,
The life-strings of that tender heart gave way;

Even sinners, taught by Thee,
40 Look Sorrow in the face,

And bid her freely welcome, unbeguiled
By false kind solaces, and spells of earth:—
And yet not all unsoothed;
For when was Joy so dear,

45 As the deep calm that breathed, "Father forgive!"
Or, "Be with Me in Paradise to-day"?
And, though the strife be sore,
Yet in His parting breath

Love masters Agony; the soul that seemed
50 Forsaken, feels her present God again,
And in her Father's arms
Contented dies away.

John Henry Newman

THE PILLAR OF THE CLOUD

THIS poem is better known by its opening line and is often sung as a hymn, but the dirge-like tune by Dykes which accompanies it hardly matches the poetic merit or brings out the spiritual struggle of Newman's acceptance of God's will. Newman wrote it before he became a Roman Catholic and while he was vicar of St. Mary's Church, Oxford. It was published in 1836 in *Lyra Apostolica*, a collection of poems by members of the Oxford Movement. In 1832 Newman visited Italy in company with his friend, Hurrell Froude, and Froude's father. The Froudes left him in Italy and returned by way of France. Newman fell dangerously ill with fever and he wrote this poem in June 1833, while still in weak health and travelling aboard ship between Palermo and Marseilles. The title is a reference to the pillar of cloud which led the Jews through the wilderness (*Exodus*, xiii).

Lead, Kindly Light, amid the encircling gloom,
    Lead Thou me on!
The night is dark, and I am far from home—
    Lead Thou me on!
5 Keep Thou my feet; I do not ask to see
The distant scene,—one step enough for me.

I was not ever thus, nor pray'd that Thou
    Shouldst lead me on.
I loved to choose and see my path; but now
10   Lead Thou me on!
I loved the garish day, and, spite of fears,
Pride ruled my will: remember not past years.

So long Thy power hath blest me, sure it still
    Will lead me on,
15 O'er moor and fen, o'er crag and torrent, till
    The night is gone;
And with the morn those angel faces smile
Which I have loved long since, and lost awhile.

from

THE DREAM OF GERONTIUS

The Dream of Gerontius, 1865, is Newman's most considerable poetic achievement. Although he had many years still before him, Newman wrote it at a time when he felt his work was at an end and his life drawing to a close. The poem begins with Gerontius on his death-bed and ends with this speech of his guardian-angel. His soul has approached the Judgement-seat and is now ready to depart for Purgatory, where it will be prepared for life with God.

ANGEL

Softly and gently, dearly-ransom'd soul,
 In my most loving arms I now enfold thee,
And, o'er the penal waters, as they roll,
 I poise thee, and I lower thee, and hold thee

5 And carefully I dip thee in the lake,
 And thou, without a sob or a resistance,
Dost through the flood thy rapid passage take,
 Sinking deep, deeper, into the dim distance.

Angels, to whom the willing task is given,
10 Shall tend, and nurse, and lull thee, as thou liest;
And Masses on the earth, and prayers in heaven,
 Shall aid thee at the Throne of the Most Highest.

Farewell, but not for ever! brother dear,
 Be brave and patient on thy bed of sorrow;
15 Swiftly shall pass thy night of trial here,
 And I will come and wake thee on the morrow.

Arthur Hugh Clough

EPI-STRAUSS-IUM

CLOUGH was one of Dr. Thomas Arnold's favourite pupils at Rugby and a friend of Matthew Arnold. From the fervent evangelical piety and moral earnestness of his home and Rugby, he went to Oxford in 1837, at a time when the university was in an intellectual ferment. Newman and his followers were at the height of their powers, but the new biblical criticism and scientific rationalism were also gaining ground. Clough lost his early faith, but he was never hostile to Christianity. His poetry is marked by a reverent scepticism, a suspension of both belief and disbelief and an attempt to see both sides of a question. He was elected to a Fellowship at Oriel College in 1842, but resigned in 1848 because he could no longer subscribe to the religious conditions which attached to it. The title of this poem can be translated as *On Straussism* and the poem is about the change in Christian belief brought about by Strauss's *Life of Jesus* (see Introduction, p. 10). At the dawn of faith the sun shines through the eastern windows of the church and shows in glowing colours the figures of the four evangelists. As the sun moves round and shines through the clear glass windows at the other side of the church, the evangelists vanish but we see things more clearly. In 1847, the year in which the poem was composed, Clough wrote: "Trust in God's justice and love, and belief in His commands as written in our conscience, stand unshaken, though Matthew, Mark, Luke, and John, or even St. Paul, were to fall."

Matthew and Mark and Luke and holy John
Evanished all and gone!
Yea, he that erst, his dusky curtains quitting,
Through Eastern pictured panes his level beams transmitting,
5 With gorgeous portraits blent,
On them his glories intercepted spent,
Southwestering now, through windows plainly glassed,
On the inside face his radiance keen hath cast,
And in the lustre lost, invisible and gone,
10 Are, say you, Matthew, Mark and Luke and holy John?
Lost, is it? lost, to be recovered never?

However,
The place of worship the meantime with light
Is, if less richly, more sincerely bright,
15 And in blue skies the Orb is manifest to sight.

EASTER DAY

Naples, 1849

This poem faces the painful consequences of a loss of Christian belief, and in places there is anger and irony, sharpened, perhaps, by the contrast between the devotion of the Italian crowds and the "sinful streets of Naples".

Through the great sinful streets of Naples as I past,
With fiercer heat than flamed above my head
My heart was hot within me; till at last
My brain was lightened, when my tongue had said

5 Christ is not risen!

Christ is not risen, no,
He lies and moulders low;
Christ is not risen.

What though the stone were rolled away, and though
10 The grave found empty there!—
If not there, then elsewhere;
If not where Joseph laid Him first, why then
Where other men
Translaid Him after; in some humbler clay
15 Long ere to-day

4 *My brain was lightened:* The intellectual problem of reconciling the "sinful streets" with a just God disappears if Christianity is not true.

12 *Joseph:* i.e. Joseph of Arimathaea (*Luke*, xxiii, 50–1). In this and the following stanzas Clough follows closely the crucifixion narrative of the various Gospels.

Corruption that sad perfect work hath done,
Which here she scarcely, lightly had begun.
The foul engendered worm
Feeds on the flesh of the life-giving form
20 Of our most Holy and Anointed One.

He is not risen, no,
He lies and moulders low;
Christ is not risen.

Ashes to ashes, dust to dust;
25 As of the unjust, also of the just—
Christ is not risen.

What if the women, ere the dawn was grey,
Saw one or more great angels, as they say,
Angels, or Him himself? Yet neither there, nor then,
30 Nor afterward, nor elsewhere, nor at all,
Hath He appeared to Peter or the Ten,
Nor, save in thunderous terror, to blind Saul;
Save in an after-Gospel and late Creed
He is not risen indeed,
35 Christ is not risen.

Or what if e'en, as runs the tale, the Ten
Saw, heard, and touched, again and yet again?

29 *Angels . . . himself:* The four gospels differ in their accounts of whom the women saw.

31 *Peter . . . Ten:* Jesus appeared to Peter on the afternoon of the first Easter Day and to the ten disciples (Judas Iscariot and Thomas were missing) in the evening (*Luke*, xxiv).

32 *Saul:* Clough refers to the conversion of St. Paul, who was struck blind by "a light from heaven" on the road to Damascus (*Acts*, ix, 3-7).

33 *Gospel . . . Creed:* The earliest Gospel, St. Mark's, was written some thirty years after the Crucifixion; the Nicene Creed was not formulated until the fourth century A.D., and the Apostles' Creed even later.

What if at Emmaüs' inn and by Capernaum's lake
Came One the bread that brake,
40 Came One that spake as never mortal spake,
And with them ate and drank and stood and walked about?
Ah! 'some' did well to 'doubt'!
Ah! the true Christ, while these things came to pass,
Nor heard, nor spake, nor walked, nor dreamt, alas!
45 He was not risen, no,
He lay and mouldered low,
Christ was not risen.

As circulates in some great city crowd
A rumour changeful, vague, importunate, and loud,
50 From no determined centre, or of fact,
Or authorship exact,
Which no man can deny
Nor verify;
So spread the wondrous fame;
55 He all the same
Lay senseless, mouldering, low.
He was not risen, no,
Christ was not risen!

Ashes to ashes, dust to dust;
60 As of the unjust, also of the just—
Yea, of that Just One too.
This is the one sad Gospel that is true,
Christ is not risen.

Is He not risen, and shall we not rise?
65 Oh, we unwise!

38 *Emmaüs . . . Capernaum:* After the Resurrection Jesus appeared to the disciples at Emmaus, a village near Jerusalem, and ate a meal with them. He also appeared to them by the sea of Galilee—"*Capernaum's lake*" (*John*, xxi, 1). St. Matthew records that some "worshipped him, but some doubted" (xxviii, 17).

What did we dream, what wake we to discover?
Ye hills, fall on us, and ye mountains, cover!
In darkness and great gloom
Come ere we thought it is *our* day of doom,
70 From the cursed world which is one tomb,
Christ is not risen!

Eat, drink, and die, for we are men deceived,
Of all the creatures under heaven's wide cope
We are most hopeless who had once most hope
75 We are most wretched that had most believed.
Christ is not risen.

Eat, drink, and play, and think that this is bliss!
There is no Heaven but this!
There is no Hell;—
80 Save Earth, which serves the purpose doubly well,
Seeing it visits still
With equallest apportionments of ill
Both good and bad alike, and brings to one same dust
The unjust and the just
85 With Christ, who is not risen.

Eat, drink, and die, for we are souls bereaved,
Of all the creatures under this broad sky
We are most hopeless, that had hoped most high,
And most beliefless, that had most believed.
90 Ashes to ashes, dust to dust;
As of the unjust, also of the just—
Yea, of that Just One too.
It is the one sad Gospel that is true,
Christ is not risen.

95 Weep not beside the Tomb,
Ye women, unto whom

73 *cope:* literally a cloak worn by the priest at church services. There may be irony in its metaphorical use here.

He was great solace while ye tended Him;
Ye who with napkin o'er His head
And folds of linen round each wounded limb
100 Laid out the Sacred Dead;
And thou that bar'st Him in thy Wondering Womb.
Yea, Daughters of Jerusalem, depart,
Bind up as best ye may your own sad bleeding heart;
Go to your homes, your living children tend,
105 Your earthly spouses love;
Set your affections *not* on things above,
Which moth and rust corrupt, which quickliest come to end:
Or pray, if pray ye must, and pray, if pray ye can,
For death; since dead is He whom ye deemed more than man,
110 Who is not risen, no,
But lies and moulders low,
Who is not risen.

Ye men of Galilee!
Why stand ye looking up to heaven, where Him ye ne'er may see,
115 Neither ascending hence, nor hither returning again?
Ye ignorant and idle fishermen!
Hence to your huts and boats and inland native shore,
And catch not men, but fish;
Whate'er things ye might wish,
120 Him neither here nor there ye e'er shall meet with more.

101 *thou that bar'st Him:* Mary, the Mother of Jesus, was amongst the women at the Tomb.

107 *moth and rust:* There is a bitter reversal here of the Sermon on the Mount in which Christ had said, "Lay up for yourselves treasures in heaven, where neither moth nor rust doth corrupt" (*Matthew*, vi, 19–20).

113–14 *Ye men . . . heaven:* At the Ascension of Jesus this question was asked of the disciples by two angels (*Acts*, i, 11). It is used with irony here.

118 *catch . . . fish:* This is another ironic inversion of the Gospel. When Jesus called Simon Peter and Andrew to be his disciples he told them to be fishers of men (*Mark*, i, 16–17).

Ye poor deluded youths, go home,
Mend the old nets ye left to roam,
Tie the split oar, patch the torn sail;
It was indeed 'an idle tale',
125 He was not risen.

And oh, good men of ages yet to be,
Who shall believe *because* ye did not see,
Oh, be ye warned! be wise!
No more with pleading eyes,
130 And sobs of strong desire,
Unto the empty vacant void aspire,
Seeking another and impossible birth
That is not of your own and only Mother Earth.
But if there is no other life for you,
135 Sit down and be content, since this must even do:
He is not risen.

One look, and then depart,
Ye humble and ye holy men of heart!
And ye! ye ministers and stewards of a word
140 Which ye would preach, because another heard,—
Ye worshippers of that ye do not know,
Take these things hence and go;
He is not risen.

Here on our Easter Day
145 We rise, we come, and lo! we find Him not;
Gardener nor other on the sacred spot,
Where they have laid Him is there none to say!
No sound, nor in, nor out; no word
Of where to seek the dead or meet the living Lord;
150 There is no glistering of an angel's wings,

146 *Gardener:* Mary Magdalene, when she first met the risen Christ, mistook him for a gardener (*John*, xx, 15).

150–1 *There . . . behest:* These lines refer to the angel who guarded Christ's sepulchre and who told the women of Christ's resurrection (*Matthew*, xxviii, 1–6).

There is no voice of heavenly clear behest:
Let us go hence, and think upon these things
In silence, which is best.
Is he not risen? No—
155 But lies and moulders low—
Christ is not risen.

EASTER DAY

II

THE date of this poem is uncertain, and we do not know whether Clough added it as an afterthought or whether it was meant to form, together with *Easter Day* (1849), one long poem. As in *Epi-Strauss-ium*, he reflects that though biblical criticism may have destroyed the historicity of the Gospel story, we still have the great meanings of Christianity as symbols of spiritual power.

So in the sinful streets, abstracted and alone,
I with my secret self held communing of mine own.
So in the southern city spake the tongue
Of one that somewhat overwildly sung;
5 But in a later hour I sat and heard
Another voice that spake, another graver word.
Weep not, it bade, whatever hath been said,
Though He be dead, He is not dead.
In the true Creed
10 He is yet risen indeed,
Christ is yet risen.

Weep not beside His tomb,
Ye women unto whom
He was great comfort and yet greater grief;
15 Nor ye faithful few that went with Him to roam,
Seek sadly what for Him ye left, go hopeless to your home;
Nor ye despair, ye sharers yet to be of their belief;
Though He be dead, He is not dead,
Not gone, though fled,

20 Not lost, though vanished;
Though He return not, though
He lies and moulders low;
In the true Creed
He is yet risen indeed,
25 Christ is yet risen.

Sit if ye will, sit down upon the ground,
Yet not to weep and wail, but calmly look around.
Whate'er befell,
Earth is not hell;
30 Now, too, as when it first began,
Life yet is Life and Man is Man.
For all that breathe beneath the heaven's high cope,
Joy with grief mixes, with despondence hope.
Hope conquers cowardice, joy grief:
35 Or at the least, faith unbelief.
Though dead, not dead;
Not gone, though fled;
Not lost, not vanished.
In the great Gospel and true Creed,
He is yet risen indeed;
40 Christ is yet risen.

Matthew Arnold

IN HARMONY WITH NATURE

To a Preacher

ARNOLD was the son of Dr. Thomas Arnold, Headmaster of Rugby, and was brought up in an atmosphere of evangelical morality and liberal Protestantism. With his friend Clough, he revolted against this upbringing while at Oxford. His revolt was compounded of a dislike of the ugliness of evangelical religion and an inability to accept the dogmas of Christianity. His advocacy of culture as a dogma-less religion and his belief that literature is a criticism of life, have been powerful influences upon literature and society in our own century. His ideal of poetry was that of the classics, and included, "as theirs did, religion with poetry, instead of existing as poetry only, and leaving religious wants to be supplied by the Christian religion". It is the human spirit at its highest, "the best that has been known and said in the world", and not science, which provides the core of Arnold's religion. In this sonnet, published in 1849, Arnold expresses his conviction that man must either transcend the natural order or be enslaved by it.

"In harmony with Nature?" Restless fool,
Who with such heat dost preach what were to thee,
When true, the last impossibility—
To be like Nature strong, like Nature cool!

5 Know, man hath all which Nature hath, but more,
And in that more lie all his hopes of good.
Nature is cruel; man is sick of blood;
Nature is stubborn; man would fain adore;

Nature is fickle; man hath need of rest;
10 Nature forgives no debt, and fears no grave;
Man would be mild, and with safe conscience blest.

Man must begin, know this, where Nature ends;
Nature and man can never be fast friends.
Fool, if thou canst not pass her, rest her slave!

TO MARGUERITE—CONTINUED

THIS is one of seven poems in a cycle entitled *Switzerland*, which Arnold published in 1852. The poems must be, in part at least, autobiographical, but Arnold was later to tell his children that Marguerite was a fictitious figure. He appears to have met this "Daughter of France" at Thun in the Bernese Oberland in 1848, but broke off the relationship in the following year. More important than the identity of Marguerite in this poem is the sense of isolation that their parting brought him. In several of his poems (e.g. the opening of *The Buried Life*) Arnold expresses this essential loneliness of human existence, and the inability even of deep love to bridge the gulf between individuals.

Yes! in the sea of life enisled,
With echoing straits between us thrown,
Dotting the shoreless watery wild,
We mortal millions live *alone*.
5 The islands feel the enclasping flow,
And then their endless bounds they know.

But when the moon their hollows lights,
And they are swept by balms of spring,
And in their glens, on starry nights,
10 The nightingales divinely sing;
And lovely notes, from shore to shore,
Across the sounds and channels pour—

Oh! then a longing like despair
Is to their farthest caverns sent;
15 For surely once, they feel, we were
Parts of a single continent!
Now round us spreads the watery plain—
Oh might our marges meet again!

Who order'd, that their longing's fire
20 Should be, as soon as kindled, cool'd?
Who renders vain their deep desire?—
A God, a God their severance ruled!
And bade betwixt their shores to be
The unplumb'd, salt, estranging sea.

22 *God:* The word here means no more than destiny or fate.

THE BURIED LIFE

THIS poem, first published in 1852, takes up the theme of *To Marguerite—Continued*, man's isolation and inability to communicate with others, and extends it to include man's ignorance of his own inner self. We all have "an unspeakable desire/After the knowledge of our buried life," but the mystery of our own identity and destiny eludes us. Arnold suffered all his life from a melancholy which not only was the product of his loss of faith and the pressures of external forces, but which issued from his own personality and his desire to come to terms with it.

Light flows our war of mocking words, and yet,
Behold, with tears mine eyes are wet!
I feel a nameless sadness o'er me roll.
Yes, yes, we know that we can jest,
5 We know, we know that we can smile!
But there's a something in this breast,
To which thy light words bring no rest,
And thy gay smiles no anodyne.
Give me thy hand, and hush awhile,
10 And turn those limpid eyes on mine,
And let me read there, love! thy inmost soul.

Alas! is even love too weak
To unlock the heart, and let it speak?
Are even lovers powerless to reveal
15 To one another what indeed they feel?
I knew the mass of men conceal'd
Their thoughts, for fear that if reveal'd
They would by other men be met
With blank indifference, or with blame reproved;
20 I knew they lived and moved
Trick'd in disguises, alien to the rest
Of men, and alien to themselves—and yet
The same heart beats in every human breast!
But we, my love!—doth a like spell benumb
25 Our hearts, our voices?—must we too be dumb?

Ah! well for us, if even we,
Even for a moment, can get free
Our heart, and have our lips unchain'd;
For that which seals them hath been deep-ordain'd!
30 Fate, which foresaw
How frivolous a baby man would be—
By what distractions he would be possess'd,
How he would pour himself in every strife,
And well-nigh change his own identity—
35 That it might keep from his capricious play
His genuine self, and force him to obey
Even in his own despite his being's law,
Bade through the deep recesses of our breast
The unregarded river of our life
40 Pursue with indiscernible flow its way;
And that we should not see
The buried stream, and seem to be
Eddying at large in blind uncertainty,
Though driving on with it eternally.

45 But often, in the world's most crowded streets,
But often, in the din of strife,
There rises an unspeakable desire
After the knowledge of our buried life;
A thirst to spend our fire and restless force
50 In tracking out our true, original course;
A longing to inquire
Into the mystery of this heart which beats
So wild, so deep in us—to know
Whence our lives come and where they go.
55 And many a man in his own breast then delves,
But deep enough, alas! none ever mines.
And we have been on many thousand lines,
And we have shown, on each, spirit and power;
But hardly have we, for one little hour,
60 Been on our own line, have we been ourselves—
Hardly had skill to utter one of all

The nameless feelings that course through our breast,
But they course on for ever unexpress'd.
And long we try in vain to speak and act
65 Our hidden self, and what we say and do
Is eloquent, is well—but 'tis not true!
And then we will no more be rack'd
With inward striving, and demand
Of all the thousand nothings of the hour
70 Their stupefying power;
Ah yes, and they benumb us at our call!
Yet still, from time to time, vague and forlorn
From the soul's subterranean depth upborne
As from an infinitely distant land,
75 Come airs, and floating echoes, and convey
A melancholy into all our day.

Only—but this is rare—
When a belovéd hand is laid in ours,
When, jaded with the rush and glare
80 Of the interminable hours,
Our eyes can in another's eyes read clear,
When our world-deafen'd ear
Is by the tones of a loved voice caress'd—
A bolt is shot back somewhere in our breast,
An air of coolness plays upon his face
85 And a lost pulse of feeling stirs again.
The eye sinks inward, and the heart lies plain,
And what we mean, we say, and what we would, we know.
A man becomes aware of his life's flow,

66 *not true:* not in accordance with our own nature.

69 *thousand nothings:* petty distractions which we use as a drug to silence our questionings.

77–90 *Only . . . breeze:* This stanza suggests that the nearest we get to understanding our true nature is in loving and being loved.

And hears its winding murmur; and he sees
90 The meadows where it glides, the sun, the breeze.

And there arrives a lull in the hot race
Wherein he doth for ever chase
That flying and elusive shadow, rest.
An air of coolness plays upon his face
95 And an unwonted calm pervades his breast.
And then he thinks he knows
The hills where his life rose,
And the sea where it goes.

DOVER BEACH

FIRST published in 1867. Nowhere in Victorian poetry are the sadness and regret at lost faith expressed more plangently than in this poem. Again Arnold finds human love the only anodyne against the pain and uncertainty of human existence.

The sea is calm to-night.
The tide is full, the moon lies fair
Upon the straits;—on the French coast the light
Gleams and is gone; the cliffs of England stand,
5 Glimmering and vast, out in the tranquil bay.
Come to the window, sweet is the night-air!
Only, from the long line of spray
Where the sea meets the moon-blanch'd land,
Listen! you hear the grating roar
10 Of pebbles which the waves draw back, and fling,
At their return, up the high strand,
Begin, and cease, and then again begin,
With tremulous cadence slow, and bring
The eternal note of sadness in.

15 Sophocles long ago

15 *Sophocles:* Greek tragic dramatist, 495-406 B.C. The reference is probably to his *Antigone*, 583 ff.

Heard it on the Ægæan, and it brought
Into his mind the turbid ebb and flow
Of human misery; we
Find also in the sound a thought,
20 Hearing it by this distant northern sea.

The Sea of Faith
Was once, too, at the full, and round earth's shore
Lay like the folds of a bright girdle furl'd.
But now I only hear
25 Its melancholy, long, withdrawing roar,
Retreating, to the breath
Of the night-wind, down the vast edges drear
And naked shingles of the world.

Ah, love, let us be true
30 To one another! for the world, which seems
To lie before us like a land of dreams,
So various, so beautiful, so new,
Hath really neither joy, nor love, nor light,
Nor certitude, nor peace, nor help for pain;
35 And we are here as on a darkling plain
Swept with confused alarms of struggle and flight,
Where ignorant armies clash by night.

George Eliot

O MAY I JOIN THE CHOIR INVISIBLE

GEORGE ELIOT (Mary Ann Evans) is best known as a novelist, and few people read or are even aware of her poetry. Her literary genius found its fittest expression in the novel, for she is concerned above all with character and the operation of the moral consciousness. But her novels reveal a sensitive appreciation of atmosphere and scenery, and a poetic imagination that reveals itself not only in the creation of characters, but in the way she relates them to their surroundings. George Eliot illustrates Victorian agnosticism at its best. Brought up in an evangelical Christian home, she lost her faith but put in its place a religion of humanity at the centre of which was a strong sense of duty. F. W. H. Myers, in a well-known passage in his *Essays—Modern* (1883), describes meeting George Eliot in Cambridge. "I remember," he writes,

> how, at Cambridge, I walked with her once in the Fellows' Garden at Trinity, on an evening of rainy May; and she . . . taking as her text the three words which have been used so often as the inspiring trumpet-calls of men,—the words *God*, *Immortality*, *Duty*,—pronounced, with terrible earnestness, how inconceivable was the *first*, how unbelievable the *second*, and yet how peremptory and absolute the *third*. Never, perhaps, have sterner accents affirmed the sovereignty of impersonal and unrecompensing Law. . . . And when we stood at length and parted, . . . I seemed to be gazing . . . on a sanctuary with no Presence to hallow it, and heaven left lonely of a God.

In this poem, written in 1867, George Eliot asks for an immortality that is no more than the moral influence of her life on generations that succeed her. The Latin motto from Cicero at the head of the poem can be translated, "That long span of years when I shall no longer be, moves me more than this brief life-span."

Longum illud tempus, quum non ero, magis me movet, quam hoc exiguum.—Cicero, *ad Att.*, xii, 18.

O may I join the choir invisible
Of those immortal dead who live again
In minds made better by their presence: live

In pulses stirred to generosity,
5 In deeds of daring rectitude, in scorn
For miserable aims that end with self,
In thoughts sublime that pierce the night like stars,
And with their mild persistence urge man's search
To vaster issues.

10 So to live is heaven:
To make undying music in the world,
Breathing as beauteous order that controls
With growing sway the growing life of man.
So we inherit that sweet purity
15 For which we struggled, failed, and agonized
With widening retrospect that bred despair.
Rebellious flesh that would not be subdued,
A vicious parent shaming still its child
Poor anxious penitence, is quick dissolved;
20 Its discords, quenched by meeting harmonies,
Die in the large and charitable air.
And all our rarer, better, truer self,
That sobbed religiously in yearning song,
That watched to ease the burthen of the world,
25 Laboriously tracing what must be,
And what may yet be better—saw within
A worthier image for the sanctuary,
And shaped it forth before the multitude
Divinely human, raising worship so
30 To higher reverence more mixed with love—
That better self shall live till human Time
Shall fold its eyelids, and the human sky
Be gathered like a scroll within the tomb
Unread for ever.

35 This is life to come,
Which martyred men have made more glorious
For us who strive to follow. May I reach
That purest heaven, be to other souls

The cup of strength in some great agony,
40 Enkindle generous ardor, feed pure love,
Beget the smiles that have no cruelty—
Be the sweet presence of a good diffused,
And in diffusion ever more intense.
So shall I join the choir invisible
45 Whose music is the gladness of the world.

Alfred, Lord Tennyson

from

IN MEMORIAM A.H.H.

In Memoriam, which was published in 1850, commemorates the death in 1833 of Tennyson's friend, Arthur Hallam. The 131 sections of the poem, of which only a selection is printed here, were written between Hallam's death and 1849. In accordance with the elegiac tradition, Tennyson not only expresses personal grief at the loss of his friend, but endeavours to reconcile the facts of death and sorrow with a belief in providence. The poet traces his own progress from despair to peace of mind and hope, but in doing so he describes the spiritual struggle of his age; issues of science, the foundations of Christian belief, and the insignificance of man in an apparently indifferent universe. The poem is not a theodicy, that is, it does not argue a belief in God in philosophical terms; it is the story of the poet's spiritual pilgrimage, what Tennyson called "the way of the soul". Tennyson was fully aware of the difficulties that beset Christian belief in his day, and was concerned to establish a faith that could embrace new knowledge and not disregard it. If his attempt to give a religious interpretation to evolutionary theory strikes us as too facile, we should remember that it was the outcome of deep agonising, and that he, too, came to discard such an interpretation (see *Locksley Hall, Sixty Years After* and Introduction, p. 22). Of the sections that follow, the first is in the form of an introduction which Tennyson wrote in 1849, when he had finished the rest of the poem. These stanzas proclaim his faith in a God of Love and Justice, who grants us free will and immortality. We cannot prove the existence of this God, by intellectual means, but if we have faith in him, this will illuminate our understanding, and faith will grow. The remaining sections printed here form a passage which runs from sections 50 to 58 of the poem. Section 50 is an anguished prayer for communion with Hallam, and this is followed (51–3) by misgivings about the poet's own worthlessness and whether this will prevent re-union with his friend. Sections 54–6 extend this doubt and ask whether love has any significance in a universe which seems to disregard it. Sections 57–8 end on a note of subdued resignation, but leave these questions unanswered.

Strong Son of God, immortal Love,
Whom we, that have not seen thy face,
By faith, and faith alone, embrace,
Believing where we cannot prove;

5 Thine are these orbs of light and shade;
Thou madest Life in man and brute;
Thou madest Death; and lo, thy foot
Is on the skull which thou hast made.

Thou wilt not leave us in the dust:
10 Thou madest man, he knows not why,
He thinks he was not made to die;
And thou hast made him: thou art just.

Thou seemest human and divine,
The highest, holiest manhood, thou:
15 Our wills are ours, we know not how;
Our wills are ours, to make them thine.

Our little systems have their day;
They have their day and cease to be:
They are but broken lights of thee,
20 And thou, O Lord, art more than they.

We have but faith: we cannot know;
For knowledge is of things we see;
And yet we trust it comes from thee,
A beam in darkness: let it grow.

17 *systems:* i.e. intellectual and social systems.

25 Let knowledge grow from more to more,
But more of reverence in us dwell;
That mind and soul, according well,
May make one music as before,

But vaster. We are fools and slight;
30 We mock thee when we do not fear:
But help thy foolish ones to bear;
Help thy vain worlds to bear thy light.

Forgive what seem'd my sin in me;
What seem'd my worth since I began;
35 For merit lives from man to man,
And not from man, O Lord, to thee.

Forgive my grief for one removed,
Thy creature, whom I found so fair.
I trust he lives in thee, and there
40 I find him worthier to be loved.

Forgive these wild and wandering cries,
Confusions of a wasted youth;
Forgive them where they fail in truth,
And in thy wisdom make me wise.

50

45 Be near me when my light is low,
When the blood creeps, and the nerves prick
And tingle; and the heart is sick,
And all the wheels of Being slow.

Be near me when the sensuous frame
50 Is rack'd with pangs that conquer trust;
And Time, a maniac scattering dust,
And Life, a Fury slinging flame.

45 *Be near . . .*: This and the following lines are addressed to Hallam.

Be near me when my faith is dry,
    And men the flies of latter spring,
55   That lay their eggs, and sting and sing
And weave their petty cells and die.

Be near me when I fade away,
    To point the term of human strife,
    And on the low dark verge of life
60 The twilight of eternal day.

51

Do we indeed desire the dead
    Should still be near us at our side?
    Is there no baseness we would hide?
No inner vileness that we dread?

65 Shall he for whose applause I strove,
    I had such reverence for his blame,
    See with clear eye some hidden shame
And I be lessen'd in his love?

I wrong the grave with fears untrue:
70   Shall love be blamed for want of faith?
    There must be wisdom with great Death:
The dead shall look me thro' and thro'.

Be near us when we climb or fall:
    Ye watch, like God, the rolling hours
75   With larger other eyes than ours,
To make allowance for us all.

52

I cannot love thee as I ought,
    For love reflects the thing beloved;
    My words are only words, and moved
80 Upon the topmost froth of thought.

54 *And men . . .:* i.e. men are like flies whose life is transitory

"Yet blame not thou thy plaintive song,"
The Spirit of true love replied;
"Thou canst not move me from thy side,
Nor human frailty do me wrong.

85 "What keeps a spirit wholly true
To that ideal which he bears?
What record? not the sinless years
That breathed beneath the Syrian blue:

"So fret not, like an idle girl,
90 That life is dash'd with flecks of sin.
Abide: thy wealth is gather'd in,
When Time hath sunder'd shell from pearl."

53

How many a father have I seen,
A sober man, among his boys,
95 Whose youth was full of foolish noise,
Who wears his manhood hale and green:

And dare we to this fancy give,
That had the wild oat not been sown,
The soil, left barren, scarce had grown
100 The grain by which a man may live?

Or, if we held the doctrine sound
For life outliving heats of youth,
Yet who would preach it as a truth
To those that eddy round and round?

105 Hold thou the good: define it well:
For fear divine Philosophy

88 *Syrian blue:* i.e. not even the life of Christ (in Syria) keeps a man true to his ideal.

Should push beyond her mark, and be
Procuress to the Lords of Hell.

54

Oh yet we trust that somehow good
110 Will be the final goal of ill,
To pangs of nature, sins of will,
Defects of doubt, and taints of blood;

That nothing walks with aimless feet;
That not one life shall be destroy'd,
115 Or cast as rubbish to the void,
When God hath made the pile complete;

That not a worm is cloven in vain;
That not a moth with vain desire
Is shrivell'd in a fruitless fire,
120 Or but subserves another's gain.

Behold, we know not anything;
I can but trust that good shall fall
At last—far off—at last, to all,
And every winter change to spring.

125 So runs my dream: but what am I?
An infant crying in the night:
An infant crying for the light:
And with no language but a cry.

55

The wish, that of the living whole
130 No life may fail beyond the grave,
Derives it not from what we have
The likest God within the soul?

108 The meaning of this section is that one should hold fast to the good; folly, both intellectual and otherwise, does not necessarily give place to wisdom.

132 *The likest . . . soul:* i.e. Love, which has a longing for immortality.

Are God and Nature then at strife,
That Nature lends such evil dreams?
135 So careful of the type she seems,
So careless of the single life;

That I, considering everywhere
Her secret meaning in her deeds,
And finding that of fifty seeds
140 She often brings but one to bear,

I falter where I firmly trod,
And falling with my weight of cares
Upon the great world's altar-stairs
That slope thro' darkness up to God,

145 I stretch lame hands of faith, and grope,
And gather dust and chaff, and call
To what I feel is Lord of all,
And faintly trust the larger hope.

56

"So careful of the type?" but no.
150 From scarped cliff and quarried stone
She cries, "A thousand types are gone:
I care for nothing, all shall go.

"Thou makest thine appeal to me:
I bring to life, I bring to death:
155 The spirit does but mean the breath:
I know no more." And he, shall he,

Man, her last work, who seem'd so fair,
Such splendid purpose in his eyes,

135 *type:* species.
150 *scarped cliff:* an escarpment; especially here a break in the cliffs where fossil remains are found.

Who roll'd the psalm to wintry skies,
160 Who built him fanes of fruitless prayer,

Who trusted God was love indeed
And love Creation's final law—
Tho' Nature, red in tooth and claw
With ravine, shriek'd against his creed—

165 Who loved, who suffer'd countless ills,
Who battled for the True, the Just,
Be blown about the desert dust,
Or seal'd within the iron hills?

No more? A monster then, a dream,
170 A discord. Dragons of the prime,
That tare each other in their slime,
Were mellow music match'd with him.

O life as futile, then, as frail!
O for thy voice to soothe and bless!
175 What hope of answer, or redress?
Behind the veil, behind the veil.

57

Peace; come away: the song of woe
Is after all an earthly song:
Peace; come away: we do him wrong
180 To sing so wildly: let us go.

170 *discord:* The meaning of this stanza is that if man is just one of an endless sequence of species, there is a discord between his dreams of survival and his physical fate. Primeval dragons do not reveal such a discord and their being would be harmonious compared with man's.

Come; let us go: your cheeks are pale;
But half my life I leave behind:
Methinks my friend is richly shrined;
But I shall pass; my work will fail.

185 Yet in these ears, till hearing dies,
One set slow bell will seem to toll
The passing of the sweetest soul
That ever look'd with human eyes.

I hear it now, and o'er and o'er,
190 Eternal greetings to the dead;
And "Ave, Ave, Ave," said,
"Adieu, adieu" for evermore.

58

In those sad words I took farewell:
Like echoes in sepulchral halls,
195 As drop by drop the water falls
In vaults and catacombs, they fell;

And, falling, idly broke the peace
Of hearts that beat from day to day,
Half-conscious of their dying clay,
200 And those cold crypts where they shall cease.

The high Muse answer'd: "Wherefore grieve
Thy brethren with a fruitless tear?
Abide a little longer here,
And thou shalt take a nobler leave."

181 *your cheeks:* This and the preceding lines are addressed to his companion at Hallam's grave.

191 *Ave:* the Latin word "Hail". This and the following line recall the lament for his dead brother by Catullus—"*Frater ave atque vale*". Tennyson used the words as the title of a poem on the death of his own brother, Charles.

LOCKSLEY HALL

TENNYSON considered *Locksley Hall* and *Locksley Hall, Sixty Years After* to be two of his most important poems and interesting as an illustration of the change in the temper of the age which had come about in his own life-time. *Locksley Hall* was written in the 1830's when the Victorian age was full of optimism. The country was entering a period of industrial expansion and the Reform Bill heralded a mood of political buoyancy. The hero of the poem is a rather Byronic figure, jilted by his cousin, Amy, for a richer suitor; rejecting the materialistic values of his own society, he considers solving his difficulties by going to the Far East or some tropical island. But in the end he feels he must serve his own country and make his contribution to the new age that is coming. See *Locksley Hall, Sixty Years After* and Introduction, pp. 22–3.

Comrades, leave me here a little, while as yet 'tis early morn:
Leave me here, and when you want me, sound upon the bugle-horn.

'Tis the place, and all around it, as of old, the curlews call,
Dreary gleams about the moorland flying over Locksley Hall;

5 Locksley Hall, that in the distance overlooks the sandy tracts,
And the hollow ocean-ridges roaring into cataracts.

Many a night from yonder ivied casement, ere I went to rest,
Did I look on great Orion sloping slowly to the West.

Many a night I saw the Pleiads, rising thro' the mellow shade,
10 Glitter like a swarm of fire-flies tangled in a silver braid.

Here about the beach I wander'd, nourishing a youth sublime
With the fairy tales of science, and the long result of Time;

When the centuries behind me like a fruitful land reposed;
When I clung to all the present for the promise that it closed;

8 *Orion:* a constellation that forms the figure of Orion, the hunter.
9 *Pleiads:* a group of small stars in the constellation Taurus.

15 When I dipt into the future far as human eye could see;
Saw the Vision of the world, and all the wonder that would be.—

In the Spring a fuller crimson comes upon the robin's breast;
In the Spring the wanton lapwing gets himself another crest;

In the Spring a livelier iris changes on the burnish'd dove;
20 In the Spring a young man's fancy lightly turns to thoughts of love.

Then her cheek was pale and thinner than should be for one so young
And her eyes on all my motions with a mute observance hung.

And I said, "My cousin Amy, speak, and speak the truth to me,
Trust me, cousin, all the current of my being sets to thee."

25 On her pallid cheek and forehead came a colour and a light,
As I have seen the rosy red flushing in the northern night.

And she turn'd—her bosom shaken with a sudden storm of sighs—
All the spirit deeply dawning in the dark of hazel eyes—

Saying, "I have hid my feelings, fearing they should do me wrong;"
30 Saying, "Dost thou love me, cousin?" weeping, "I have loved thee long."

Love took up the glass of Time, and turn'd it in his glowing hands;
Every moment, lightly shaken, ran itself in golden sands.

Love took up the harp of Life, and smote on all the chords with might;
Smote the chord of Self, that, trembling, pass'd in music out of sight.

35 Many a morning on the moorland did we hear the copses ring,
And her whisper throng'd my pulses with the fulness of the Spring.

Many an evening by the waters did we watch the stately ships,
And our spirits rush'd together at the touching of the lips.

O my cousin, shallow-hearted! O my Amy, mine no more!
40 O the dreary, dreary moorland! O the barren, barren shore!

Falser than all fancy fathoms, falser than all songs have sung,
Puppet to a father's threat, and servile to a shrewish tongue!

Is it well to wish thee happy?—having known me—to decline
On a range of lower feelings and a narrower heart than mine!

45 Yet it shall be: thou shalt lower to his level day by day,
What is fine within thee growing coarse to sympathise with clay.

As the husband is, the wife is: thou art mated with a clown,
And the grossness of his nature will have weight to drag thee down.

He will hold thee, when his passion shall have spent its novel force,
50 Something better than his dog, a little dearer than his horse.

What is this? his eyes are heavy: think not they are glazed with wine.
Go to him: it is thy duty: kiss him: take his hand in thine.

It may be my lord is weary, that his brain is overwrought:
Soothe him with thy finer fancies, touch him with thy lighter thought.

55 He will answer to the purpose, easy things to understand—
Better thou wert dead before me, tho' I slew thee with my hand!

Better thou and I were lying, hidden from the heart's disgrace,
Roll'd in one another's arms, and silent in a last embrace.

Cursed be the social wants that sin against the strength of youth!
60 Cursed be the social lies that warp us from the living truth!

Cursed be the sickly forms that err from honest Nature's rule!
Cursed be the gold that gilds the straiten'd forehead of the fool!

Well—'tis well that I should bluster!—Hadst thou less unworthy proved—
Would to God—for I had loved thee more than ever wife was loved.

65 Am I mad, that I should cherish that which bears but bitter fruit?
I will pluck it from my bosom, tho' my heart be at the root.

Never, tho' my mortal summers to such length of years should come
As the many-winter'd crow that leads the clanging rookery home.

Where is comfort? in division of the records of the mind?
70 Can I part her from herself, and love her, as I knew her, kind?

I remember one that perish'd: sweetly did she speak and move:
Such a one do I remember, whom to look at was to love.

Can I think of her as dead and love her for the love she bore?
No—she never loved me truly: love is love for evermore.

68 *crow:* The names *rook* and *crow* were interchangeable in Lincolnshire.

75 Comfort? comfort scorn'd of devils! This is truth the poet sings,
That a sorrow's crown of sorrow is remembering happier things.

Drug thy memories, lest thou learn it, lest thy heart be put to proof,
In the dead unhappy night, and when the rain is on the roof.

Like a dog, he hunts in dreams, and thou art staring at the wall,
80 Where the dying night-lamp flickers, and the shadows rise and fall.

Then a hand shall pass before thee, pointing to his drunken sleep,
To thy widow'd marriage-pillows, to the tears that thou wilt weep.

Thou shalt hear the "Never, never", whisper'd by the phantom years,
And a song from out the distance in the ringing of thine ears;

85 And an eye shall vex thee, looking ancient kindness on thy pain.
Turn thee, turn thee on thy pillow: get thee to thy rest again.

Nay, but Nature brings thee solace; for a tender voice will cry.
'Tis a purer life than thine; a lip to drain thy trouble dry.

Baby lips will laugh me down: my latest rival brings thee rest.
90 Baby fingers, waxen touches, press me from the mother's breast.

O, the child too clothes the father with a dearness not his due.
Half is thine and half is his: it will be worthy of the two.

75 *the poet:* Dante (*Inferno*, V, 121).

O, I see thee old and formal, fitted to thy petty part,
With a little hoard of maxims preaching down a daughter's heart.

95 "They were dangerous guides the feelings—she herself was not exempt—
Truly, she herself had suffer'd"—Perish in thy self-contempt!

Overlive it—lower yet—be happy! wherefore should I care?
I myself must mix with action, lest I wither by despair.

What is that which I should turn to, lighting upon days like these?
100 Every door is barr'd with gold, and opens but to golden keys.

Every gate is throng'd with suitors, all the markets overflow.
I have but an angry fancy: what is that which I should do?

I had been content to perish, falling on the foeman's ground,
When the ranks are roll'd in vapour, and the winds are laid with sound.

105 But the jingling of the guinea helps the hurt that Honour feels,
And the nations do but murmur, snarling at each other's heels.

Can I but relive in sadness? I will turn that earlier page.
Hide me from my deep emotion, O thou wondrous Mother-Age!

Make me feel the wild pulsation that I felt before the strife,
110 When I heard my days before me, and the tumult of my life;

97 *Overlive it:* i.e. subdue his sorrow by attending to the business of living.
104 *vapour* i.e. gunsmoke.

Yearning for the large excitement that the coming years would yield
Eager-hearted as a boy when first he leaves his father's field,

And at night along the dusky highway near and nearer drawn,
Sees in heaven the light of London flaring like a dreary dawn;

115 And his spirit leaps within him to be gone before him then,
Underneath the light he looks at, in among the throngs of men:

Men, my brothers, men the workers, ever reaping something new:
That which they have done but earnest of the things that they shall do:

For I dipt into the future, far as human eye could see,
120 Saw the Vision of the world, and all the wonder that would be;

Saw the heavens fill with commerce, argosies of magic sails,
Pilots of the purple twilight, dropping down with costly bales;

Heard the heavens fill with shouting, and there rain'd a ghastly dew
From the nations' airy navies grappling in the central blue;

125 Far along the world-wide whisper of the south-wind rushing warm,
With the standards of the peoples plunging thro' the thunder-storm;

Till the war-drum throbb'd no longer and the battle-flags were furl'd
In the Parliament of man, the Federation of the world.

There the common sense of most shall hold a fretful realm in awe,
130 And the kindly earth shall slumber, lapt in universal law.

So I triumph'd ere my passion sweeping thro' me left me dry,
Left me with the palsied heart, and left me with the jaundiced eye;

Eye, to which all order festers, all things here are out of joint:
Science moves, but slowly slowly, creeping on from point to point:

135 Slowly comes a hungry people, as a lion creeping nigher,
Glares at one that nods and winks behind a slowly-dying fire,

Yet I doubt not thro' the ages one increasing purpose runs,
And the thoughts of men are widen'd with the process of the suns.

What is that to him that reaps not harvest of his youthful joys,
140 Tho' the deep heart of existence beat for ever like a boy's?

Knowledge comes, but wisdom lingers, and I linger on the shore,
And the individual withers, and the world is more and more.

Knowledge comes, but wisdom lingers, and he bears a laden breast,
Full of sad experience, moving toward the stillness of his rest.

145 Hark, my merry comrades call me, sounding on the bugle-horn,
They to whom my foolish passion were a target for their scorn:

142 *world:* i.e. a political system which favours the masses rather than the individual.

Shall it not be scorn to me to harp on such a moulder'd string?
I am shamed thro' all my nature to have loved so slight a thing.

Weakness to be wroth with weakness! woman's pleasure, woman's pain—
150 Nature made them blinder motions bounded in a shallower brain:

Woman is the lesser man, and all thy passions, match'd with mine,
Are as moonlight unto sunlight, and as water unto wine—

Here at least, where nature sickens, nothing. Ah, for some retreat
Deep in yonder shining Orient, where my life began to beat;

155 Where in wild Mahratta-battle fell my father evil-starr'd;—
I was left a trampled orphan, and a selfish uncle's ward.

Or to burst all links of habit—there to wander far away,
On from island unto island at the gateways of the day.

Larger constellations burning, mellow moons and happy skies,
160 Breadths of tropic shade and palms in cluster, knots of Paradise.

Never comes the trader, never floats an European flag,
Slides the bird o'er lustrous woodland, swings the trailer from the crag;

Droops the heavy-blossom'd bower, hangs the heavy-fruited tree—
Summer isles of Eden lying in dark-purple spheres of sea.

155 *Mahratta:* Lord Hastings defeated the Indian Mahrattas in 1818.
162 *trailer:* creeping vegetation.

165 There methinks would be enjoyment more than in this march of mind,
In the steamship, in the railway, in the thoughts that shake mankind.

There the passions cramp'd no longer shall have scope and breathing space;
I will take some savage woman, she shall rear my dusky race.

Iron jointed, supple-sinew'd, they shall dive, and they shall run,
170 Catch the wild goat by the hair, and hurl their lances in the sun;

Whistle back the parrot's call, and leap the rainbows of the brooks,
Not with blinded eyesight poring over miserable books—

Fool, again the dream, the fancy! but I know my words are wild,
But I count the gray barbarian lower than the Christian child.

175 I, to herd with narrow foreheads, vacant of our glorious gains,
Like a beast with lower pleasures, like a beast with lower pains!

Mated with a squalid savage—what to me were sun or clime?
I the heir of all the ages, in the foremost files of time—

I that rather held it better men should perish one by one,
180 Than that earth should stand at gaze like Joshua's moon in Ajalon!

171 *rainbows:* caused by the sun shining on the spray.

180 *Joshua:* Joshua commanded the moon to stand still at Ajalon (*Joshua*, x, 12-13).

Not in vain the distance beacons. Forward, forward let us range,
Let the great world spin for ever down the ringing grooves of change.

Thro' the shadow of the globe we sweep into the younger day:
Better fifty years of Europe than a cycle of Cathay.

185 Mother-Age (for mine I knew not) help me as when life begun:
Rift the hills, and roll the waters, flash the lightnings, weigh the Sun.

O, I see the crescent promise of my spirit hath not set.
Ancient founts of inspiration well thro' all my fancy yet.

Howsoever these things be, a long farewell to Locksley Hall!
190 Now for me the woods may wither, now for me the roof-tree fall.

Comes a vapour from the margin, blackening over heath and holt,
Cramming all the blast before it, in its breast a thunderbolt.

Let it fall on Locksley Hall, with rain or hail, or fire or snow;
For the mighty wind arises, roaring seaward, and I go.

182 *grooves:* When Tennyson wrote this line railways were still an innovation. The poet, who was short-sighted, thought that railway wheels ran in grooves, instead of having flanges.

LOCKSLEY HALL, SIXTY YEARS AFTER

In this poem, written in 1886, the speaker is the same hero as in *Locksley Hall*, but now grown into an old man. His youthful optimism and hope have largely faded. The political promises of the Reform Bill have been unfulfilled, the prospect of peace either at home or abroad seems unlikely, and the brave claims of science now seem an empty boast. The old man is revisiting Locksley Hall for the funeral of his old rival, Amy's husband. Amy herself has been dead these many years, as has his own wife, Edith.

His only son has been drowned at sea, but he meets at Locksley his grandson, who is heir to the estate, and who, to repeat history, has been jilted too. Though many of his youthful aspirations have been dashed, the old man is not merely cynical. He realises that Amy's husband, dull and limited as he was, had many of the qualities he himself lacks: regard for tradition, care for his estate and employees, and stability. His anger and contempt for his old rival have vanished, and have been replaced by the belief that "Love will conquer in the end", the note on which the poem finishes. See Introduction, pp. 22–3.

Late, my grandson! half the morning have I paced these sandy tracts,
Watch'd again the hollow ridges roaring into cataracts,

Wander'd back to living boyhood while I heard the curlews call,
I myself so close on death, and death itself in Locksley Hall.

5 So—your happy suit was blasted—she the faultless, the divine;
And you liken—boyish babble—this boy-love of yours with mine.

I myself have often babbled doubtless of a foolish past;
Babble, babble; our old England may go down in babble at last.

"Curse him!" curse your fellow-victim? call him dotard in your rage?
10 Eyes that lured a doting boyhood well might fool a dotard's age.

Jilted for a wealthier! wealthier? yet perhaps she was not wise;
I remember how you kiss'd the miniature with those sweet eyes.

In the hall there hangs a painting—Amy's arms about my neck—
Happy children in a sunbeam sitting on the ribs of wreck.

15 In my life there was a picture, she that clasp'd my neck had flown;
I was left within the shadow sitting on the wreck alone.

Yours has been a slighter ailment, will you sicken for her sake?
You, not you! your modern amourist is of easier, earthlier make.

Amy loved me, Amy fail'd me, Amy was a timid child;
20 But your Judith—but your worldling—*she* had never driven me wild.

She that holds the diamond necklace dearer than the golden ring,
She that finds a winter sunset fairer than a morn of Spring.

She that in her heart is brooding on his briefer lease of life,
While she vows "till death shall part us," she the would-be-widow wife.

25 She the wordling born of worldlings—father, mother—be content,
Ev'n the homely farm can teach us there is something in descent.

Yonder in that chapel, slowly sinking now into the ground,
Lies the warrior, my forefather, with his feet upon the hound.

Cross'd! for once he sail'd the sea to crush the Moslem in his pride;
30 Dead the warrior, dead his glory, dead the cause in which he died.

Yet how often I and Amy in the mouldering aisle have stood,
Gazing for one pensive moment on that founder of our blood.

29 *Cross'd:* The crossing of the feet signified that he had been a Crusader. The figure of a favourite hound was often placed at the foot of an effigy.

There again I stood to-day, and where of old we knelt in prayer,
Close beneath the casement crimson with the shield of Locksley—there,

35 All in white Italian marble, looking still as if she smiled,
Lies my Amy dead in child-birth, dead the mother, dead the child.

Dead—and sixty years ago, and dead her aged husband now—
I this old white-headed dreamer stoopt and kiss'd her marble brow.

Gone the fires of youth, the follies, furies, curses, passionate tears,
40 Gone like fires and floods and earthquakes of the planet's dawning years.

Fires that shook me once, but now to silent ashes fall'n away.
Cold upon the dead volcano sleeps the gleam of dying day.

Gone the tyrant of my youth, and mute below the chancel stones,
All his virtues—I forgive them—black in white above his bones.

45 Gone the comrades of my bivouac, some in fight against the foe,
Some thro' age and slow diseases, gone as all on earth will go.

Gone with whom for forty years my life in golden sequence ran,
She with all the charm of woman, she with all the breadth of man,

Strong in will and rich in wisdom, Edith, yet so lowly-sweet,
50 Woman to her inmost heart, and woman to her tender feet,

43 *tyrant:* Amy's father, who forbade her match with the hero.
45 *comrades:* The speaker had joined the army after being jilted.

Very woman of very woman, nurse of ailing body and mind,
She that link'd again the broken chain that bound me to my kind.

Here to-day was Amy with me, while I wander'd down the coast,
Near us Edith's holy shadow, smiling at the slighter ghost.

55 Gone our sailor son thy father, Leonard, early lost at sea;
Thou alone, my boy, of Amy's kin and mine art left to me.

Gone thy tender-natured mother, wearying to be left alone,
Pining for the stronger heart that once had beat beside her own.

Truth, for Truth is Truth, he worshipt, being true as he was brave;
60 Good, for Good is Good, he follow'd, yet he look'd beyond the grave,

Wiser there than you, that crowning barren Death as lord of all,
Deem this over-tragic drama's closing curtain is the pall!

Beautiful was death in him, who saw the death, but kept the deck,
Saving women and their babes, and sinking with the sinking wreck,

65 Gone for ever! Ever? no—for since our dying race began,
Ever, ever, and for ever was the leading light of man.

Those that in barbarian burials kill'd the slave, and slew the wife
Felt within themselves the sacred passion of the second life.

67 In this and the following lines the speaker suggests that even savage people had a belief in immortality.

Indian warriors dream of ampler hunting grounds beyond the night;
70 Ev'n the black Australian dying hopes he shall return, a white.

Truth for truth, and good for good! The Good, the True, the Pure, the Just—
Take the charm "For ever" from them, and they crumble into dust.

Gone the cry of "Forward, Forward," lost within a growing gloom;
Lost, or only heard in silence from the silence of a tomb.

75 Half the marvels of my morning, triumphs over time and space,
Staled by frequence, shrunk by usage into commonest commonplace!

"Forward" rang the voices then, and of the many mine was one.
Let us hush this cry of "Forward" till ten thousand years have gone.

Far among the vanish'd races, old Assyrian kings would flay
80 Captives whom they caught in battle—iron-hearted victors they.

Ages after, while in Asia, he that led the wild Moguls,
Timur, built his ghastly tower of eighty thousand human skulls,

Then, and here in Edward's time, an age of noblest English names,
Christian conquerors took and flung the conquer'd Christian into flames.

82 *Timur:* The same as Tamerlane, a fourteenth-century Tartar, who invaded India and Asia.

83 *Edward's time:* This and the next line presumably refer to Edward III and the start of the Hundred Years War.

85 Love your enemy, bless your haters, said the Greatest of the great;
Christian love among the Churches look'd the twin of heathen hate.

From the golden alms of Blessing man had coin'd himself a curse:
Rome of Caesar, Rome of Peter, which was crueller? which was worse?

France had shown a light to all men, preach'd a Gospel, all men's good;
90 Celtic Demos rose a Demon, shriek'd and slaked the light with blood.

Hope was ever on her mountain, watching till the dawn begun—
Crown'd with sunlight—over darkness—from the still unrisen sun.

Have we grown at last beyond the passions of the primal clan?
"Kill your enemy, for you hate him," still, "your enemy" was a man.

95 Have we sunk below them? peasants maim the helpless horse, and drive
Innocent cattle under thatch, and burn the kindlier brutes alive.

Brutes, the brutes are not your wrongers—burnt at midnight, found at morn,
Twisted hard in mortal agony with their offspring, born-unborn,

90 *Celtic Demos:* The allusion is to the French Revolution. "Demos" literally means "people", but "Celtic" is an inexact description of the French.

95-6 These lines refer to the atrocities in nineteenth-century Ireland during the eviction of peasants from their lands.

Clinging to the silent mother! Are we devils? are we men?
100 Sweet St. Francis of Assisi, would that he were here again,

He that in his Catholic wholeness used to call the very flowers
Sisters, brothers—and the beasts—whose pains are hardly less than ours!

Chaos, Cosmos! Cosmos, Chaos! who can tell how all will end?
Read the wide world's annals, you, and take their wisdom for your friend.

105 Hope the best, but hold the Present fatal daughter of the Past,
Shape your heart to front the hour, but dream not that the hour will last.

Ay, if dynamite and revolver leave you courage to be wise:
When was age so cramm'd with menace? madness? written, spoken lies?

Envy wears the mask of Love, and, laughing sober fact to scorn,
110 Cries to Weakest as to Strongest, "Ye are equals, equal-born."

Equal-born? O yes, if yonder hill be level with the flat.
Charm us, Orator, till the Lion look no larger than the Cat,

Till the Cat thro' that mirage of overheated language loom
Larger than the Lion,—Demos end in working its own doom.

115 Russia bursts our Indian barrier, shall we fight her? shall we yield?
Pause! before you sound the trumpet, hear the voices from the field.

115 This refers to border incidents on the North-West Frontier of India in Tennyson's time.

Those three hundred millions under one Imperial sceptre now,
Shall we hold them? shall we loose them? take the suffrage of the plow.

Nay, but these would feel and follow Truth if only you and you,
120 Rivals of realm-ruining party, when you speak were wholly true.

Plowmen, Shepherds, have I found, and more than once, and still could find
Sons of God, and kings of men in utter nobleness of mind,

Truthful, trustful, looking upward to the practised hustings-liar;
So the Higher wields the Lower, while the Lower is the Higher.

125 Here and there a cotter's babe is royal-born by right divine;
Here and there my lord is lower than his oxen or his swine.

Chaos, Cosmos! Cosmos, Chaos! once again the sickening game;
Freedom, free to slay herself, and dying while they shout her name.

Step by step we gain'd a freedom known to Europe, known to all;
130 Step by step we rose to greatness,—thro' the tonguesters we may fall.

You that woo the Voices—tell them "old experience is a fool,"
Teach your flatter'd kings that only those who cannot read can rule.

123 *hustings-liar:* i.e. parliamentary candidate (hustings being the platform on which the parliamentary candidate stood).

Pluck the mighty from their seat, but set no meek ones in their place;
Pillory Wisdom in your markets, pelt your offal at her face.

135 Tumble Nature heel o'er head, and, yelling with the yelling street,
Set the feet above the brain and swear the brain is in the feet.

Bring the old dark ages back without the faith, without the hope,
Break the State, the Church, the Throne, and roll their ruins down the slope.

Authors—essayist, atheist, novelist, realist, rhymester, play your part,
140 Paint the mortal shame of nature with the living hues of Art.

Rip your brothers' vices open, strip your own foul passions bare;
Down with Reticence, down with Reverence—forward—naked—let them stare.

Feed the budding rose of boyhood with the drainage of your sewer;
Send the drain into the fountain, lest the stream should issue pure.

145 Set the maiden fancies wallowing in the troughs of Zolaism,—
Forward, forward, ay and backward, downward too into the abysm.

Do your best to charm the worst, to lower the rising race of men;
Have we risen from out the beast, then back into the beast again?

145 *Zolaism:* Emile Zola, a French nineteenth-century novelist, some of whose works depict the seamier side of life.

Only "dust to dust" for me that sicken at your lawless din,
150 Dust in wholesome old-world dust before the newer world begin.

Heated am I? you—you wonder—well, it scarce becomes mine age—
Patience! let the dying actor mouth his last upon the stage.

Cries of unprogressive dotage ere the dotard fall asleep?
Noises of a current narrowing, not the music of a deep?

155 Ay, for doubtless I am old, and think gray thoughts, for I am gray:
After all the stormy changes shall we find a changeless May?

After madness, after massacre, Jacobinism and Jacquerie,
Some diviner force to guide us thro' the days I shall not see?

When the schemes and all the systems, Kingdoms and Republics fall,
160 Something kindlier, higher, holier—all for each and each for all?

All the full-brain, half-brain races, led by Justice, Love, and Truth;
All the millions one at length with all the visions of my youth?

All diseases quench'd by Science, no man halt, or deaf or blind;
Stronger ever born of weaker, lustier body, larger mind?

154 *current narrowing:* i.e. the stream of life is running out and narrowing.

157 *Jacobinism and Jacquerie:* The Jacobins were a group of extreme radicals at the time of the French Revolution. *Jacquerie* is a collective name for the French peasantry.

165 Earth at last a warless world, a single race, a single tongue—
I have seen her far away—for is not Earth as yet so young?—

Every tiger madness muzzled, every serpent passion kill'd,
Every grim ravine a garden, every blazing desert till'd,

Robed in universal harvest up to either pole she smiles,
170 Universal ocean softly washing all her warless Isles.

Warless? when her tens are thousands, and her thousands millions, then—
All her harvest all too narrow—who can fancy warless men?

Warless? war will die out late then. Will it ever? late or soon?
Can it, till this outworn earth be dead as yon dead world the moon?

175 Dead the new astronomy calls her. . . . On this day and at this hour,
In this gap between the sandhills, whence you see the Locksley tower,

Here we met, our latest meeting—Amy—sixty years ago—
She and I—the moon was falling greenish thro' a rosy glow,

Just above the gateway tower, and even where you see her now—
180 Here we stood and claspt each other, swore the seeming-deathless vow . . .

Dead, but how her living glory lights the hall, the dune, the grass!
Yet the moonlight is the sunlight, and the sun himself will pass.

Venus near her! smiling downward at this earthlier earth of ours,
Closer on the Sun, perhaps a world of never fading flowers.

185 Hesper, whom the poet call'd the Bringer home of all good things.
All good things may move in Hesper, perfect peoples, perfect kings.

Hesper—Venus—were we native to that splendour or in Mars,
We should see the Globe we groan in, fairest of their evening stars.

Could we dream of wars and carnage, craft and madness, lust and spite,
190 Roaring London, raving Paris, in that point of peaceful light?

Might we not in glancing heavenward on a star so silver-fair,
Yearn, and clasp the hands and murmur, "Would to God that we were there"?

Forward, backward, backward, forward, in the immeasurable sea,
Sway'd by vaster ebbs and flows than can be known to you or me.

195 All the suns—are these but symbols of innumerable man,
Man or Mind that sees a shadow of the planner or the plan?

Is there evil but on earth? or pain in every peopled sphere?
Well, be grateful for the sounding watchword "Evolution" here,

Evolution ever climbing after some ideal good,
200 And Reversion ever dragging Evolution in the mud.

What are men that He should heed us? cried the king of sacred song;
Insects of an hour, that hourly work their brother insect wrong,

185 *Hesper:* the evening star.
201 *king of sacred song:* King David, the Psalmist (see *Psalms*, viii, 4).

While the silent Heavens roll, and Suns along their fiery way,
All their planets whirling round them, flash a million miles a day.

205 Many an Æon moulded earth before her highest, man, was born,
Many an Æon too may pass when earth is manless and forlorn,

Earth so huge, and yet so bounded—pools of salt, and plots of land—
Shallow skin of green and azure—chains of mountain, grains of sand!

Only That which made us, meant us to be mightier by and by,
210 Set the sphere of all the boundless Heavens within the human eye,

Sent the shadow of Himself, the boundless, thro' the human soul;
Boundless inward, in the atom, boundless outward, in the Whole.

* * * * *

Here is Locksley Hall, my grandson, here the lion-guarded gate.
Not to-night in Locksley Hall—to-morrow—you, you come so late.

215 Wreck'd—your train—or all but wreck'd? a shatter'd wheel? a vicious boy!
Good, this forward, you that preach it, is it well to wish you joy?

Is it well that while we range with Science, glorying in the Time,
City children soak and blacken soul and sense in city slime?

205 *Æon:* age.

There among the glooming alleys Progress halts on palsied feet,
220 Crime and hunger cast our maidens by the thousand on the street.

There the Master scrimps his haggard sempstress of her daily bread,
There a single sordid attic holds the living and the dead.

There the smouldering fire of fever creeps across the rotted floor,
And the crowded couch of incest in the warrens of the poor.

225 Nay, your pardon, cry your "forward", yours are hope and youth, but I
Eighty winters leave the dog too lame to follow with the cry,

Lame and old, and past his time, and passing now into the night;
Yet I would the rising race were half as eager for the light.

Light the fading gleam of Even? light the glimmer of the dawn?
230 Aged eyes may take the growing glimmer for the gleam withdrawn.

Far away beyond her myriad coming changes earth will be
Something other than the wildest modern guess of you and me.

Earth may reach her earthly-worst; or if she gain her earthly-best,
Would she find her human offspring this ideal man at rest?

221-2 Charles Kingsley had drawn attention to the sweated conditions in the tailoring trade in his novel *Alton Locke* (1850).

235 Forward then, but still remember how the course of Time will swerve,
Crook and turn upon itself in many a backward streaming curve.

Not the Hall to-night, my grandson! Death and Silence hold their own.
Leave the Master in the first dark hour of his last sleep alone.

Worthier soul was he than I am, sound and honest, rustic Squire,
240 Kindly landlord, boon companion—youthful jealousy is a liar.

Cast the poison from your bosom, oust the madness from your brain.
Let the trampled serpent show you that you have not lived in vain.

Youthful! youth and age are scholars yet but in the lower school,
Nor is he the wisest man who never proved himself a fool.

245 Yonder lies our young sea-village—Art and Grace are less and less:
Science grows and Beauty dwindles—roofs of slated hideousness!

There is one old Hostel left us where they swing the Locksley shield,
Till the peasant cow shall butt the "Lion passant" from his field.

242 *trampled serpent:* i.e. the slain dragon of evil.

247 *Host-el:* i.e. the village inn.

248 i.e. the power of the working classes shall have replaced that of the aristocracy.

Poor old Heraldry, poor old History, poor old Poetry, passing hence,
250 In the common deluge drowning old political common-sense!

Poor old voice of eighty crying after voices that have fled!
All I loved are vanish'd voices, all my steps are on the dead.

All the world is ghost to me, and as the phantom disappears,
Forward far and far from here is all the hope of eighty years.

* * * * *

255 In this Hostel!—I remember—I repent it o'er his grave—
Like a clown—by chance he met me—I refused the hand he gave.

From that casement where the trailer mantles all the mouldering bricks—
I was then in early boyhood, Edith but a child of six—

While I sheltered in this archway from a day of driving showers—
260 Peept the winsome face of Edith like a flower among the flowers.

Here to-night! the Hall to-morrow, when they toll the Chapel bell!
Shall I hear in one dark room a wailing, "I have loved thee well."

Then a peal that shakes the portal—one has come to claim his bride,
Her that shrank, and put me from her, shriek'd, and started from my side—

257 *trailer:* creeper.

265 Silent echoes! You, my Leonard, use and not abuse your day,
Move among your people, know them, follow him who led the way,

Strove for sixty widow'd years to help his homelier brother men,
Served the poor, and built the cottage, raised the school, and drain'd the fen.

Hears he now the Voice that wrong'd him? who shall swear it cannot be?
270 Earth would never touch her worst, were one in fifty such as he.

Ere she gain her Heavenly-best, a God must mingle with the game:
Nay, there may be those about us whom we neither see nor name,

Felt within us as ourselves, the Powers of Good, the Powers of Ill,
Strowing balm, or shedding poison in the fountains of the Will.

275 Follow you the Star that lights a desert pathway, yours or mine.
Forward, till you see the highest Human Nature is divine.

Follow Light, and do the Right—for man can half-control his doom—
Till you find the deathless Angel seated in the vacant tomb.

Forward, let the stormy moment fly and mingle with the Past.
280 I that loathed, have come to love him. Love will conquer at the last.

278 *deathless Angel:* See *Mark*, xvi, 5.

Gone at eighty, mine own age, and I and you will bear the pall;
Then I leave thee Lord and Master, latest Lord of Locksley Hall.

CROSSING THE BAR

WRITTEN in 1889, three years before the poet's death. Tennyson asked that this poem should always be printed at the end of his works. He wrote the first draft of the poem while crossing the Solent on his way to his home at Farringford in the Isle of Wight.

Sunset and evening star,
And one clear call for me!
And may there be no moaning of the bar,
When I put out to sea,

5 But such a tide as moving seems asleep,
Too full for sound and foam,
When that which drew from out the boundless deep
Turns again home.

Twilight and evening bell,
10 And after that the dark!
And may there be no sadness of farewell,
When I embark;

For tho' from out our bourne of Time and Place
The flood may bear me far,
15 I hope to see my Pilot face to face
When I have crost the bar.

15 The ship is outward bound and the pilot has been on board from the start of the voyage. Now that the difficult task of leaving harbour (symbolising death) is past, the voyager at last comes face to face with the pilot.

Robert Browning

SAUL

BROWNING published this poem in the second volume of *Men and Women*, 1855, but the first nine stanzas had already appeared in *Bells and Pomegranates*, 1845. The poem is based upon the story, in *I Samuel*, xvi, 14-23, of how David played the harp to King Saul to dispel the deep depression which had settled on him. At first, David plays the songs he knows as a shepherd; then the folk-songs of the Jewish people, songs that celebrate the harvest, funerals and marriages, and the priest at the altar. He tries to make the king aware of the blessings of life; parents, family, health and strength. The king gradually begins to emerge from his melancholy, but David looks to something that will sustain him even after the song has finished. So David passes to thoughts of immortality; his love for the king and his desire to help him evoke a vision of the nature and destiny of man. If David's love for the king is ready to embrace even suffering on his behalf, will not God's love for us be even greater than this? David the harpist becomes David the prophet, who proclaims, "See the Christ stand!"

I

Said Abner, "At last thou art come! Ere I tell, ere thou speak,
Kiss my cheek, wish me well!" Then I wished it, and did kiss his cheek.
And he, "Since the King, O my friend, for thy countenance sent,
Neither drunken nor eaten have we; nor until from his tent
5 Thou return with the joyful assurance the King liveth yet,
Shall our lip with the honey be bright, with the water be wet
For out of the black mid-tent's silence, a space of three days,
Not a sound hath escaped to thy servants, of prayer or of praise,
To betoken that Saul and the Spirit have ended their strife,
10 And that, faint in his triumph, the monarch sinks back upon life.

1 *Abner:* the captain of Saul's army.

9 *Spirit:* ". . . an evil spirit from the Lord troubled him" (*I Samuel*, xvi, 14).

II

Yet now my heart leaps, O beloved! God's child, with his dew
On thy gracious gold hair, and those lilies still living and blue
Just broken to twine round thy harp-strings, as if no wild heat
Were now raging to torture the desert!"

III

Then I, as was meet,
15 Knelt down to the God of my fathers, and rose on my feet,
And ran o'er the sand burnt to powder. The tent was unlooped;
I pulled up the spear that obstructed, and under I stooped;
Hands and knees on the slippery grass-patch, all withered and gone,
That extends to the second enclosure, I groped my way on
20 Till I felt where the foldskirts fly open. Then once more I prayed,
And opened the foldskirts and entered, and was not afraid,
But spoke, "Here is David, thy servant!" And no voice replied.
At the first I saw nought but the blackness; but soon I descried
A something more black than the blackness—the vast, the upright
25 Main prop which sustains the pavilion: and slow into sight
Grew a figure against it, gigantic and blackest of all:
Then a sunbeam, that burst thro' the tent-roof, showed Saul.

IV

He stood as erect as that tent-prop; both arms stretched out wide
On the great cross-support in the centre, that goes to each side:
30 He relaxed not a muscle, but hung there, as, caught in his pangs
And waiting his change the king-serpent all heavily hangs,

Far away from his kind, in the pine, till deliverance come
With the spring-time,—so agonized Saul, drear and stark, blind and dumb.

V

Then I tuned my harp,—took off the lilies we twine round its chords
35 Lest they snap 'neath the stress of the noontide—those sunbeams like swords!
And I first played the tune all our sheep know, as, one after one,
So docile they come to the pen-door, till folding be done.
They are white and untorn by the bushes, for lo, they have fed
Where the long grasses stifle the water within the stream's bed;
40 And now one after one seeks its lodging, as star follows star
Into eve and the blue far above us,—so blue and so far!

VI

—Then the tune, for which quails on the cornland will each leave his mate
To fly after the player; then, what makes the crickets elate,
Till for boldness they fight one another: and then, what has weight
45 To set the quick jerboa a-musing outside his sand house—
There are none such as he for a wonder, half bird and half mouse!—
God made all the creatures and gave them our love and our fear,
To give sign, we and they are His children, one family here.

VII

Then I played the help-tune of our reapers, their wine-song, when hand

45 *jerboa:* a little desert rodent.
49 *help-tune:* tune played at a rustic festival.

50 Grasps at hand, eye lights eye in good friendship, and great hearts expand
And grow one in the sense of this world's life.—And then, the last song
When the dead man is praised on his journey—"Bear, bear him along
With his few faults shut up like dead flowerets! are balm-seeds not here
To console us? The land has none left, such as he on the bier.
55 Oh, would we might keep thee, my brother!"—And then, the glad chaunt
Of the marriage,—first go the young maidens, next, she whom we vaunt
As the beauty, the pride of our dwelling.—And then, the great march
Wherein man runs to man to assist him and buttress an arch
Nought can break; who shall harm them, our friends?—Then, the chorus intoned
60 As the Levites go up to the altar in glory enthroned.
But I stopped here—for here in the darkness, Saul groaned.

VIII

And I paused, held my breath in such silence, and listened apart;
And the tent shook, for mighty Saul shuddered—and sparkles 'gan dart
From the jewels that woke in his turban at once with a start—
65 All its lordly male-sapphires, and rubies courageous at heart.
So the head—but the body still moved not, still hung there erect.
And I bent once again to my playing, pursued it unchecked,
As I sang,—

60 *Levites:* one of the tribes of Israel which traditionally provided the Jewish priests.

65 *male-sapphires:* superior sapphires.

IX

"Oh, our manhood's prime vigour! no spirit feels waste,
Not a muscle is stopped in its playing, nor sinew unbraced.
70 Oh, the wild joys of living! the leaping from rock up to rock—
The strong rending of boughs from the fir-tree,—the cool silver shock
Of the plunge in a pool's living water,—the hunt of the bear,
And the sultriness showing the lion is couched in his lair.
And the meal—the rich dates yellowed over with gold dust divine,
75 And the locust's-flesh steeped in the pitcher! the full draught of wine,
And the sleep in the dried river-channel where bulrushes tell
That the water was wont to go warbling so softly and well.
How good is man's life, the mere living! how fit to employ
All the heart and the soul and the senses, for ever in joy!
80 Hast thou loved the white locks of thy father, whose sword thou didst guard
When he trusted thee forth with the armies, for glorious reward?
Didst thou see the thin hands of thy mother, held up as men sung
The low song of the nearly-departed, and heard her faint tongue
Joining in while it could to the witness, "Let one more attest,
85 I have lived, seen God's hand thro' a lifetime, and all was for best"?
Then they sung thro' their tears in strong triumph, not much —but the rest.
And thy brothers, the help and the contest, the working whence grew
Such results as, from seething grape-bundles, the spirit strained true!

86 *not much—but the rest:* the little that remained unsaid.

And the friends of thy boyhood—that boyhood of wonder
and hope,
90 Present promise, and wealth of the future beyond the eye's
scope,—
Till lo, thou art grown to a monarch; a people is thine;
And all gifts, which the world offers singly, on one head
combine!
On one head, all the beauty and strength, love and rage (like
the throe
That, a-work in the rock, helps its labour and lets the gold go)
95 High ambition and deeds which surpass it, fame crowning
it,—all
Brought to blaze on the head of one creature—King Saul!"

X

And lo, with that leap of my spirit,—heart, hand, harp and
voice,
Each lifting Saul's name out of sorrow, each bidding rejoice
Saul's fame in the light it was made for—as when, dare I say,
100 The Lord's army, in rapture of service, strains through its
array,
And upsoareth the cherubim-chariot—"Saul!" cried I, and
stopped,
And waited the thing that should follow. Then Saul, who
hung propt
By the tent's cross-support in the centre, was struck by his
name.
Have ye seen when Spring's arrowy summons goes right to
the aim,
105 And some mountain, the last to withstand her, that held (he
alone,

93 *throe:* a violent convulsion preceding the bringing forth of something.

98 *Saul's name:* The word "name" in the Old Testament often means a person's spirit or real nature.

101 *cherubim-chariot:* The throne of God is often represented in the Old Testament as a chariot drawn by cherubim (e.g. *Ezekiel*, x).

104 *arrowy summons:* i.e. shafts of sunshine.

While the vale laughed in freedom and flowers) on a broad bust of stone
A year's snow bound about for a breastplate,—leaves grasp of the sheet?
Fold on fold all at once it crowds thunderously down to his feet,
And there fronts you, stark, black, but alive yet, your mountain of old,
110 With his rents, the successive bequeathings of ages untold—
Yea, each harm got in fighting your battles, each furrow and scar
Of his head thrust 'twixt you and the tempest—all hail, there they are!
Now again to be softened with verdure, again hold the nest
Of the dove, tempt the goat and its young to the green on its crest
115 For their food in the ardours of summer! One long shudder thrilled
All the tent till the very air tingled, then sank and was stilled
At the King's self left standing before me, released and aware.
What was gone, what remained? all to traverse 'twixt hope and despair;
Death was past, life not come: so he waited. Awhile his right hand
120 Held the brow, helped the eyes left too vacant forthwith to remand
To their place what new objects should enter: 'twas Saul as before.
I looked up and dared gaze at those eyes, nor was hurt any more
Than by slow pallid sunsets in autumn, ye watch from the shore,

107 *sheet:* i.e. the covering of snow. The poet is comparing Saul to a snow-covered mountain which is being laid bare by spring sunshine. The melted snow crashes down in an avalanche.

118 *hope and despair:* Saul is shaking off his lethargy, but it is still uncertain whether he will renounce despair and choose hope.

At their sad level gaze o'er the ocean—a sun's slow decline
125 Over hills which, resolved in stern silence, o'erlap and entwine
Base with base to knit strength more intense: so, arm folded in arm
O'er the chest whose slow heavings subsided.

XI

What spell or what charm,
(For, awhile there was trouble within me) what next should I urge
To sustain him where song had restored him?—Song filled to the verge
130 His cup with the wine of this life, pressing all that it yields
Of mere fruitage, the strength and the beauty! Beyond, on what fields,
Glean a vintage more potent and perfect to brighten the eye
And bring blood to the lip, and commend them the cup they put by?
He saith, "It is good;" still he drinks not; he lets me praise life,
135 Gives assent, yet would die for his own part.

XII

Then fancies grew rife
Which had come long ago on the pastures, when round me the sheep
Fed in silence—above, the one eagle wheeled slow as in sleep,
And I lay in my hollow, and mused on the world that might lie
'Neath his ken, though I saw but the strip 'twixt the hill and the sky:
140 And I laughed—"Since my days are ordained to be passed with my flocks,
Let me people at least, with my fancies, the plains and the rocks,
Dream the life I am never to mix with, and image the show
Of mankind as they live in those fashions I hardly shall know!

Schemes of life, its best rules and right uses, the courage that gains,
145 And the prudence that keeps what men strive for." And now these old trains
Of vague thought came again; I grew surer; so once more the string
Of my harp made response to my spirit, as thus—

XIII

"Yea, my king,"
I began—"thou dost well in rejecting mere comforts that spring
From the mere mortal life held in common by man and by brute:
150 In our flesh grows the branch of this life, in our soul it bears fruit.
Thou hast marked the slow rise of the tree,—how its stem trembled first
Till it passed the kid's lip, the stag's antler; then safely outburst
The fan-branches all round; and thou mindest when these too, in turn
Broke a-bloom and the palm-tree seemed perfect; yet more was to learn
155 Ev'n the good that comes in with the palm-fruit. Our dates shall we slight,
When their juice brings a cure for all sorrow? or care for the plight
Of the palm's self whose slow growth produced them? Not so! stem and branch
Shall decay nor be known in their place, while the palm-wine shall staunch
Every wound of man's spirit in winter. I pour thee such wine.
160 Leave the flesh to the fate it was fit for! the spirit be thine!
By the spirit, when age shall o'ercome thee, thou still shalt enjoy
More indeed, than at first when inconscious, the life of a boy.

Crush that life, and behold its wine running! each deed thou hast done
Dies, revives, goes to work in the world; until e'en as the sun
165 Looking down on the earth, though clouds spoil him, though tempests efface,
Can find nothing his own deed produced not, must everywhere trace
The results of his past summer-prime,—so, each ray of thy will,
Every flash of thy passion and prowess, long over, shall thrill
Thy whole people, the countless, with ardour, till they too give forth
170 A like cheer to their sons, who in turn, fill the South and the North
With the radiance thy deed was the germ of. Carouse in the Past!
But the license of age has its limit; thou diest at last:
As the lion when age dims his eyeball, the rose at her height,
So with man—so his power and his beauty for ever take flight.
175 No! again a long draught of my soul-wine! look forth o'er the years—
Thou hast done now with eyes for the actual; begin with the seer's!
Is Saul dead? in the depth of the vale make his tomb—bid arise
A grey mountain of marble heaped four-square, till, built to the skies,
Let it mark where the great First King slumbers: whose fame would ye know?
180 Up above see the rock's naked face, where the record shall go
In great characters cut by the scribe,—Such was Saul, so he did;
With the sages directing the work, by the populace chid,—

171 *Carouse in the Past!:* i.e. memories of youthful prowess are a legitimate pleasure, but age necessarily takes their place.

179 *First King:* Saul was the first king of Israel.

For not half, they'll affirm, is comprised there! Which fault to amend,
In the grove with his kind grows the cedar, whereon they shall spend
185 (See, in tablets 'tis level before them) their praise, and record
With the gold of the graver, Saul's story,—the statesman's great word
Side by side with the poet's sweet comment. The river's a-wave
With smooth paper-reeds grazing each other when prophet-winds rave:
So the pen gives unborn generations their due and their part
190 In thy being! Then, first of the mighty, thank God that thou art."

XIV

And behold while I sang . . . But O Thou who didst grant me that day,
And before it not seldom, hast granted Thy help to essay,
Carry on and complete an adventure,—my Shield and my Sword
In that act where my soul was Thy servant, Thy word was my word,—
195 Still be with me, who then at the summit of human endeavour
And scaling the highest, man's thought could, gazed hopeless as ever
On the new stretch of Heaven above me—till, mighty to save,
Just one lift of Thy hand cleared that distance—God's throne from man's grave!
Let me tell out my tale to its ending—my voice to my heart
200 Which can scarce dare believe in what marvels last night I took part,

188 *paper-reeds:* i.e. the papyrus plants growing on the river banks seem almost aware of their destiny in providing the means of recording Saul's achievements.

199 *my voice to my heart:* i.e. may my song express the feelings in my heart.

As this morning I gather the fragments, alone with my sheep,
And still fear lest the terrible glory evanish like sleep!
For I wake in the grey dewy covert, while Hebron upheaves
The dawn struggling with night on his shoulder, and Kidron retrieves
205 Slow the damage of yesterday's sunshine.

XV

I say then,—my song
While I sang thus, assuring the monarch, and ever more strong
Made a proffer of good to console him—he slowly resumed
His old motions and habitudes kingly. The right hand replumed
His black locks to their wonted composure, adjusted the swathes
210 Of his turban, and see—the huge sweat that his countenance bathes,
He wipes off with the robe; and he girds now his loins as of yore
And feels slow for the armlets of price, with the clasp set before.
He is Saul, ye remember in glory,—ere error had bent
The broad brow from the daily communion; and still, though much spent
215 Be the life and the bearing that front you, the same, God did choose,
To receive what a man may waste, desecrate, never quite lose.
So sank he along by the tent-prop, till, stayed by the pile
Of his armour and war-cloak and garments he leaned there awhile,
And so sat out my singing,—one arm round the tent-prop, to raise
220 His bent head, and the other hung slack—till I touched on the praise

203 *Hebron:* a city to the south of Jerusalem.
204 *Kidron:* a brook near Jerusalem.

I foresaw from all men in all times, to the man patient there;
And thus ended the harp falling forward. Then first I was 'ware
That he sat, as I say, with my head just above his vast knees
Which were thrust out on each side around me, like oak-roots which please
225 To encircle a lamb when it slumbers. I looked up to know
If the best I could do had brought solace: he spoke not, but slow
Lifted up the hand slack at his side, till he laid it with care
Soft and grave, but in mild settled will, on my brow: thro' my hair
The large fingers were pushed, and he bent back my head, with kind power—
230 All my face back, intent to peruse it as men do a flower.
Thus held he me there with his great eyes that scrutinized mine—
And oh, all my heart how it loved him! but where was the sign?
I yearned—"Could I help thee, my father, inventing a bliss,
I would add to that life of the Past, both the Future and this;
235 I would give thee new life altogether, as good, ages hence,
As this moment,—had love but the warrant, love's heart to dispense!"

XVI

Then the truth came upon me. No harp more—no song more! out-broke—

XVII

"I have gone the whole round of Creation: I saw and I spoke!
I, a work of God's hand for that purpose, received in my brain
240 And pronounced on the rest of his handwork—returned him again
His creation's approval or censure: I spoke as I saw.
I report, as a man may of God's work—all's love, yet all's law!

Now I lay down the judgeship He lent me. Each faculty tasked
To perceive Him, has gained an abyss, where a dewdrop was asked.
245 Have I knowledge? confounded it shrivels at Wisdom laid bare.
Have I forethought? how purblind, how blank, to the Infinite Care!
Do I task any faculty highest, to image success?
I but open my eyes,—and perfection, no more and no less,
In the kind I imagined, full-fronts me, and God is seen God
250 In the star, in the stone, in the flesh, in the soul and the clod.
And thus looking within and around me, I ever renew
(With that stoop of the soul which in bending upraises it too)
The submission of Man's nothing-perfect to God's All-Complete,
As by each new obeisance in spirit, I climb to His feet!
255 Yet with all this abounding experience, this Deity known,
I shall dare to discover some province, some gift of my own.
There's a faculty pleasant to exercise, hard to hood-wink,
I am fain to keep still in abeyance, (I laugh as I think)
Lest, insisting to claim and parade in it, wot ye, I worst
260 E'en the Giver in one gift.—Behold! I could love if I durst!
But I sink the pretension as fearing a man may o'ertake
God's own speed in the one way of love: I abstain, for love's sake!
—What, my soul? see thus far and no farther? when doors great and small,
Nine-and-ninety flew ope at our touch, should the hundredth appal?
265 In the least things, have faith, yet distrust in the greatest of all?

244 *abyss . . . dewdrop:* David had asked for a mere dewdrop (i.e. a small favour) from God, but has been shewn an abyss (i.e. a sight of the depths of being).

260 *one gift:* i.e. love. David finds it difficult to attribute to God a love greater than his own for Saul. But then he recognises that if love is a gift from God, he cannot pretend to outdo ("worst") God in loving.

Do I find love so full in my nature, God's ultimate gift,
That I doubt His own love can compete with it? here, the parts shift?
Here, the creature surpass the Creator, the end, what Began?—
Would I fain in my impotent yearning do all for this man,
270 And dare doubt He alone shall not help him, who yet alone can?
Would it ever have entered my mind, the bare will, much less power,
To bestow on this Saul what I sang of, the marvellous dower
Of the life he was gifted and filled with? to make such a soul,
Such a body, and then such an earth for insphering the whole?
275 And doth it not enter my mind (as my warm tears attest)
These good things being given, to go on, and give one more, the best?
Ay, to save and redeem and restore him, maintain at the height
This perfection,—succeed with life's dayspring, death's minute of night?
Interpose at the difficult minute, snatch Saul, the mistake,
280 Saul, the failure, the ruin he seems now,—and bid him awake
From the dream, the probation, the prelude, to find himself set
Clear and safe in new light and new life,—a new harmony yet
To be run, and continued, and ended—who knows?—or endure!
The man taught enough by life's dream, of the rest to make sure;
285 By the pain-throb, triumphantly winning intensified bliss,
And the next world's reward and repose, by the struggles in this.

XVIII

"I believe it! 'tis Thou, God, that givest, 'tis I who receive:
In the first is the last, in Thy will is my power to believe.
All's one gift: Thou canst grant it moreover, as prompt to my prayer
290 As I breathe out this breath, as I open these arms to the air.

From Thy will, stream the worlds, life and nature, thy dread Sabaoth:
I will?—the mere atoms despise me! and why am I not loth
To look that, even that in the face too? why is it I dare
Think but lightly of such impuissance? what stops my despair?
295 This:—'tis not what man Does which exalts him, but what man Would do!
See the King—I would help him but cannot, the wishes fall through.
Could I wrestle to raise him from sorrow, grow poor to enrich,
To fill up his life, starve my own out, I would—knowing which,
I know that my service is perfect. Oh, speak through me now!
300 Would I suffer for him that I love? So wouldst Thou—so wilt Thou!
So shall crown Thee the topmost, ineffablest, uttermost crown—
And Thy love fill infinitude wholly, nor leave up nor down
One spot for the creature to stand in! It is by no breath,
Turn of eye, wave of hand, that salvation joins issue with death!
305 As Thy Love is discovered almighty, almighty be proved
Thy power, that exists with and for it, of being Beloved!
He who did most, shall bear most; the strongest shall stand the most weak.
'Tis the weakness in strength that I cry for! my flesh, that I seek
In the Godhead! I seek and I find it. O Saul, it shall be
310 A Face like my face that receives thee: a Man like to me,
Thou shalt love and be loved by, for ever: a Hand like this hand
Shall throw open the gates of new life to thee! See the Christ stand!"

291 *Sabaoth:* In Hebrew the word literally means armies or hosts.

295 *'tis not . . . Would do:* a favourite thought of Browning, expressed in several other poems.

XIX

I know not too well how I found my way home in the night.
There were witnesses, cohorts about me, to left and to right,
315 Angels, powers, the unuttered unseen, the alive, the aware—
I repressed, I got through them as hardly, as strugglingly there,
As a runner beset by the populace famished for news—
Life or death. The whole earth was awakened, hell loosed with her crews;
And the stars of night beat with emotion, and tingled and shot
320 Out in fire the strong pain of pent knowledge: but I fainted not,
For the Hand still impelled me at once and supported, suppressed
All the tumult, and quenched it with quiet, and holy behest,
Till the rapture was shut in itself, and the earth sank to rest.
Anon at the dawn, all that trouble had withered from earth—
325 Not so much, but I saw it die out in the day's tender birth;
In the gathered intensity brought to the grey of the hills;
In the shuddering forests' new awe; in the sudden wind-thrills;
In the startled wild beasts that bore off, each with eye sidling still
Though averted with wonder and dread; in the birds stiff and chill
330 That rose heavily, as I approached them, made stupid with awe!
E'en the serpent that slid away silent,—he felt the new Law.
The same stared in the white humid faces upturned by the flowers;
The same worked in the heart of the cedar, and moved the vine-bowers:
And the little brooks witnessing murmured, persistent and low,
335 With their obstinate, all but hushed voices—"E'en so, it is so!"

AN EPISTLE CONTAINING THE STRANGE MEDICAL EXPERIENCE OF KARSHISH, THE ARAB PHYSICIAN

THIS poem, published in 1855, is in the form of a letter from Karshish to his teacher, Abib. The scene is Bethany, near Jerusalem, the village where nearly forty years earlier Jesus had raised Lazarus from the dead (*John*, xi, 1-44). Karshish represents the sceptical, scientific mind which tries to account in natural terms for a phenomenon it cannot comprehend. Karshish explains Lazarus's story and his state of mind as "a case of mania subinduced by epilepsy". Furthermore, Karshish is an Arab for whom the whole idea of the Incarnation is scandalous. But the unearthly radiance that shines through Lazarus is such that at the end of the poem Karshish is almost driven to abandon his prejudices and make an acknowledgement of faith in the Christian God.

Karshish, the picker-up of learning's crumbs,
The not-incurious in God's handiwork
(This man's-flesh He hath admirably made,
Blown like a bubble, kneaded like a paste,
5 To coop up and keep down on earth a space
That puff of vapour from His mouth, man's soul)
—To Abib, all-sagacious in our art,
Breeder in me of what poor skill I boast,
Like me inquisitive how pricks and cracks
10 Befall the flesh through too much stress and strain,
Whereby the wily vapour fain would slip
Back and rejoin its source before the term,—
And aptest in contrivance, under God,
To baffle it by deftly stopping such:—
15 The vagrant Scholar to his Sage at home
Sends greeting (health and knowledge, fame with peace)
Three samples of true snake-stone—rarer still,

1 *Karshish:* in Arabic literally means a "picker-up of learning's crumbs".

11 *wily vapour:* i.e. the soul. Karshish believes in the pre-existence of the soul.

One of the other sort, the melon-shaped,
(But fitter, pounded fine, for charms than drugs)
20 And writeth now the twenty-second time.

My journeyings were brought to Jericho:
Thus I resume. Who studious in our art
Shall count a little labour unrepaid?
I have shed sweat enough, left flesh and bone
25 On many a flinty furlong of this land.
Also, the country-side is all on fire
With rumours of a marching hitherward:
Some say Vespasian cometh, some, his son.
A black lynx snarled and pricked a tufted ear;
30 Lust of my blood inflamed his yellow balls:
I cried and threw my staff and he was gone.
Twice have the robbers stripped and beaten me,
And once a town declared me for a spy,
But at the end, I reach Jerusalem,
35 Since this poor covert where I pass the night,
This Bethany, lies scarce the distance thence
A man with plague-sores at the third degree
Runs till he drops down dead. Thou laughest here!
'Sooth, it elates me, thus reposed and safe,
40 To void the stuffing of my travel-scrip
And share with thee whatever Jewry yields.
A viscid choler is observable
In tertians, I was nearly bold to say,
And falling-sickness hath a happier cure
45 Than our school wots of: there's a spider here

17 *snake-stone:* a stone believed to cure snake bites.

28 *Vespasian:* the Roman Emperor who had been in charge of Judea until he was made Emperor in A.D. 69. His son, Titus, attacked and captured Jerusalem in A.D. 70.

42 *viscid choler:* a sticky fluid. Choler in Greek means "bile", which was thought to produce irascibility.

43 *tertians:* a fever that recurs every other day.

44 *falling-sickness:* epilepsy.

Weaves no web, watches on the ledge of tombs,
Sprinkled with mottles on an ash-grey back;
Take five and drop them . . . but who knows his mind,
The Syrian run-a-gate I trust this to?
50 His service payeth me a sublimate
Blown up his nose to help the ailing eye.
Best wait: I reach Jerusalem at morn,
There set in order my experiences,
Gather what most deserves, and give thee all—
55 Or I might add, Judæa's gum-tragacanth
Scales off in purer flakes, shines clearer-grained,
Cracks 'twixt the pestle and the porphyry,
In fine exceeds our produce. Scalp-disease
Confounds me, crossing so with leprosy—
60 Thou hadst admired one sort I gained at Zoar—
But zeal outruns direction. Here I end.

Yet stay: my Syrian blinketh gratefully,
Protesteth his devotion is my price—
Suppose I write what harms not, though he steal?
65 I half resolve to tell thee, yet I blush,
What set me off a-writing first of all.
An itch I had, a sting to write, a tang!
For, be it this town's barrenness—or else
The Man had something in the look of him—
70 His case has struck me far more than 'tis worth.
So, pardon if—(lest presently I lose

49 *Syrian run-a-gate:* a native who has been cured of eye-trouble by Karshish. In return for the medicine (*sublimate*) prescribed, the native has promised to carry the doctor's letter. *Run-a-gate* is a corruption of M.E. *renegat* or rascal.

55 *gum-tragacanth:* a gum secreted by the tragacanth-shrub (goat's-thorn) and used in medicine as a base for drugs.

57 *porphyry:* a mortar (or perhaps just a slab) made of porphyry, in which the drug is crushed.

59 *crossing so:* i.e. complicated by leprosy.

60 *one sort:* i.e. one case of scalp-disease. Zoar was a city near the Dead Sea.

67 *tang:* a sense of excitement.

In the great press of novelty at hand
The care and pains this somehow stole from me)
I bid thee take the thing while fresh in mind,
75 Almost in sight—for, wilt thou have the truth?
The very man is gone from me but now,
Whose ailment is the subject of discourse.
Thus then, and let thy better wit help all.

'Tis but a case of mania—subinduced
80 By epilepsy, at the turning point
Of trance prolonged unduly some three days,
When, by the exhibition of some drug
Or spell, exorcization, stroke of art
Unknown to me and which 'twere well to know,
85 The evil thing out-breaking all at once
Left the man whole and sound of body indeed,—
But, flinging, so to speak, life's gates too wide,
Making a clear house of it too suddenly,
The first conceit that entered might inscribe
90 Whatever it was minded on the wall
So plainly at that vantage, as it were,
(First come, first served) that nothing subsequent
Attaineth to erase those fancy-scrawls
The just-returned and new-established soul
95 Hath gotten now so thoroughly by heart
That henceforth she will read or these or none.
And first—the man's own firm conviction rests
That he was dead (in fact they buried him)
—That he was dead and then restored to life
100 By a Nazarene physician of his tribe:
—'Sayeth, the same bade "Rise," and he did rise.
"Such cases are diurnal," thou wilt cry.
Not so this figment!—not, that such a fume,

82 *exhibition:* i.e. administration.
91 *at that vantage:* i.e. having the advantage of being the first impression.
103 *a fume:* an obsession, the origin of which is explained physiologically by Karshish as a vapour rising into the brain.

Instead of giving way to time and health,
105 Should eat itself into the life of life,
As saffron tingeth flesh, blood, bones and all!
For see, how he takes up the after-life.
The man—it is one Lazarus a Jew,
Sanguine, proportioned, fifty years of age,
110 The body's habit wholly laudable,
As much, indeed, beyond the common health
As he were made and put aside to show.
Think, could we penetrate by any drug
And bathe the wearied soul and worried flesh,
115 And bring it clear and fair, by three days' sleep!
Whence has the man the balm that brightens all?
This grown man eyes the world now like a child.
Some elders of his tribe, I should premise,
Led in their friend, obedient as a sheep,
120 To bear my inquisition. While they spoke,
Now sharply, now with sorrow,—told the case,—
He listened not except I spoke to him,
But folded his two hands and let them talk,
Watching the flies that buzzed: and yet no fool.
125 And that's a sample how his years must go.
Look if a beggar, in fixed middle-life,
Should find a treasure, can he use the same
With straitened habits and with tastes starved small,
And take at once to his impoverished brain
130 The sudden element that changes things,
That sets the undreamed-of rapture at his hand,
And puts the cheap old joy in the scorned dust?
Is he not such an one as moves to mirth—
Warily parsimonious, when no need,
135 Wasteful as drunkenness at undue times?

106 *saffron:* a product of a plant belonging to the crocus family. It was used as a medicine, and also as a dye.

107 *after-life:* the life restored to him after what Karshish regards as his illness.

109 *Sanguine:* healthy; literally "full-blooded".

All prudent counsel as to what befits
The golden mean, is lost on such an one:
The man's fantastic will is the man's law.
So here—we'll call the treasure knowledge, say,
140 Increased beyond the fleshly faculty—
Heaven opened to a soul while yet on earth,
Earth forced on a soul's use while seeing Heaven.
The man is witless of the size, the sum,
The value in proportion of all things,
145 Or whether it be little or be much.
Discourse to him of prodigious armaments
Assembled to besiege his city now,
And of the passing of a mule with gourds—
'Tis one! Then take it on the other side,
150 Speak of some trifling fact—he will gaze rapt
With stupor at its very littleness,
(Far as I see)—as if in that indeed
He caught prodigious import, whole results;
And so will turn to us the bystanders
155 In ever the same stupor (note this point)
That we too see not with his opened eyes.
Wonder and doubt come wrongly into play,
Preposterously, at cross purposes.
Should his child sicken unto death,—why, look
160 For scarce abatement of his cheerfulness,
Or pretermission of his daily craft—
While a word, gesture, glance, from that same child
At play or in the school or laid asleep,
Will startle him to an agony of fear,
165 Exasperation, just as like! demand
The reason why—" 'tis but a word," object—
"A gesture"—he regards thee as our lord
Who lived there in the pyramid alone,

143 *witless:* unaware of.
161 *pretermission:* interruption.
167 *our lord:* some wise man known to Karshish and Abib when children.

Looked at us, dost thou mind?—when being young
170 We both would unadvisedly recite
Some charm's beginning, from that book of his,
Able to bid the sun throb wide and burst
All into stars, as suns grown old are wont.
Thou and the child have each a veil alike
175 Thrown o'er your heads, from under which ye both
Stretch your blind hands and trifle with a match
Over a mine of Greek fire, did ye know!
He holds on firmly to some thread of life—
(It is the life to lead perforcedly)
180 Which runs across some vast distracting orb
Of glory on either side that meagre thread,
Which, conscious of, he must not enter yet—
The spiritual life around the earthly life!
The law of that is known to him as this—
185 His heart and brain move there, his feet stay here.
So is the man perplext with impulses
Sudden to start off crosswise, not straight on,
Proclaiming what is Right and Wrong across,
And not along, this black thread through the blaze—
190 "It should be" baulked by "here it cannot be"
And oft the man's soul springs into his face
As if he saw again and heard again
His sage that bade him "Rise" and he did rise.
Something, a word, a tick of the blood within

177 *Greek fire:* Karshish suggests that humans are like blindfolded children who might accidentally set on fire a dangerous explosive; that is, we might in our ignorance stumble on some great truth. Greek fire was an inflammable material used for setting fire to an enemy's ships.

178 *some thread of life:* For Lazarus, life is no more than a thread he must follow, but one which runs through a world of glory which is more real to him than this one.

188-90 *Proclaiming . . . cannot be:* Lazarus is living partly on the eternal side of things and views moral questions from this transcendental viewpoint, i.e. "across, and not along" the thread of mortal life he still has to follow.

195 Admonishes—then back he sinks at once
To ashes, that was very fire before,
In sedulous recurrence to his trade
Whereby he earneth him the daily bread;
And studiously the humbler for that pride,
200 Professedly the faultier that he knows
God's secret, while he holds the thread of life.
Indeed the especial marking of the man
Is prone submission to the Heavenly will—
Seeing it, what it is, and why it is.
205 'Sayeth, he will wait patient to the last
For that same death which must restore his being
To equilibrium, body loosening soul
Divorced even now by premature full growth:
He will live, nay, it pleaseth him to live
210 So long as God please, and just how God please.
He even seeketh not to please God more
(Which meaneth, otherwise) than as God please.
Hence I perceive not he affects to preach
The doctrine of his sect whate'er it be—
215 Make proselytes as madmen thirst to do:
How can he give his neighbour the real ground,
His own conviction? ardent as he is—
Call his great truth a lie, why, still the old
"Be it as God please" reassureth him.
220 I probed the sore as thy disciple should—
"How beast," said I, "this stolid carelessness
Sufficeth thee, when Rome is on her march
To stamp out like a little spark thy town,
Thy tribe, thy crazy tale and thee at once?"
225 He merely looked with his large eyes on me.
The man is apathetic, you deduce?
Contrariwise he loves both old and young,
Able and weak—affects the very brutes
And birds—how say I? flowers of the field—
230 As a wise workman recognises tools

200 *Professedly the faultier:* more conscious of his own sin.

In a master's workshop, loving what they make.
Thus is the man as harmless as a lamb:
Only impatient, let him do his best,
At ignorance and carelessness and sin—
235 An indignation which is promptly curbed:
As when in certain travels I have feigned
To be an ignoramus in our art
According to some preconceived design,
And happed to hear the land's practitioners
240 Steeped in conceit sublimed by ignorance,
Prattle fantastically on disease,
Its cause and cure—and I must hold my peace!

Thou wilt object—why have I not ere this
Sought out the sage himself, the Nazarene
245 Who wrought this cure, enquiring at the source,
Conferring with the frankness that befits?
Alas! it grieveth me, the learned leech
Perished in a tumult many years ago,
Accused,—our learning's fate,—of wizardry,
250 Rebellion, to the setting up a rule
And creed prodigious as described to me.
His death which happened when the earthquake fell
(Prefiguring, as soon appeared, the loss
To occult learning in our lord the sage
255 That lived there in the pyramid alone)
Was wrought by the mad people—that's their wont—
On vain recourse, as I conjecture it,

247 *leech:* physician.

252 *earthquake:* a reference to the earthquake which rent the veil of the temple at Christ's death (*Matthew*, xxvii, 51). In the following lines it appears either that Karshish has received a confused account of the crucifixion narrative, or that Lazarus has given him information not contained in the Gospels, for the Bible does not say that the Jews asked Christ for help against the earthquake.

253 *Prefiguring:* Christ's death for Karshish is merely a prefiguration of the death of his own Master, to him a much more important event.

To his tried virtue, for miraculous help—
How could he stop the earthquake? That's their way!
260 The other imputations must be lies:
But take one—though I loathe to give it thee,
In mere respect to any good man's fame!
(And after all our patient Lazarus
Is stark mad; should we count on what he says?
265 Perhaps not: though in writing to a leech
'Tis well to keep back nothing of a case.)
This man so cured regards the curer then,
As—God forgive me—who but God himself,
Creator and Sustainer of the world,
270 That came and dwelt in flesh on it awhile!
—'Sayeth that such an One was born and lived,
Taught, healed the sick, broke bread at his own house,
Then died, with Lazarus by, for aught I know,
And yet was . . . what I said nor choose repeat,
275 And must have so avouched himself, in fact,
In hearing of this very Lazarus
Who saith—but why all this of what he saith?
Why write of trivial matters, things of price
Calling at every moment for remark?
280 I noticed on the margin of a pool
Blue-flowering borage, the Aleppo sort,
Aboundeth, very nitrous. It is strange!

Thy pardon for this long and tedious case,
Which, now that I review it, needs must seem
285 Unduly dwelt on, prolixly set forth.
Nor I myself discern in what is writ
Good cause for the peculiar interest
And awe indeed this man has touched me with.
Perhaps the journey's end, the weariness
290 Had wrought upon me first. I met him thus—

274 Karshish breaks off here for he cannot bring himself to write about what would come next in the story, the Resurrection. He feels this would make him ridiculous to Abib.

I crossed a ridge of short sharp broken hills
Like an old lion's cheek-teeth. Out there came
A moon made like a face with certain spots
Multiform, manifold and menacing:
295 Then a wind rose behind me. So we met
In this old sleepy town at unaware,
The man and I. I send thee what is writ.
Regard it as a chance, a matter risked
To this ambiguous Syrian—he may lose,
300 Or steal, or give it thee with equal good.
Jerusalem's repose shall make amends
For time this letter wastes, thy time and mine;
Till when, once more thy pardon and farewell!

The very God! think, Abib; dost thou think?
305 So, the All-Great, were the All-Loving too—
So, through the thunder comes a human voice
Saying, "O heart I made, a heart beats here!
Face, My hands fashioned, see it in Myself.
Thou hast no power nor may'st conceive of Mine,
310 But love I gave thee, with Myself to love,
And thou must love Me who have died for thee!"
The madman saith He said so: it is strange.

304 Having dismissed Lazarus and his story, Karshish cannot refrain from adding a postscript which reveals the tremendous impact made upon him by what he has recorded.

BISHOP BLOUGRAM'S APOLOGY

FIRST published in *Men and Women*, vol. I, 1855. Browning admitted that he modelled Bishop Blougram on Cardinal Wiseman, who became the first Archbishop of Westminster and head of the Roman Catholic Church in England when the Roman Catholic hierarchy was restored in 1850. Wiseman was a brilliant, worldly and sophisticated ecclesiastic, and some readers of the poem have seen it as simply a satirical portrait of the Archbishop. Others have regarded it as a sardonic commentary upon Roman Catholicism itself. Neither of these interpretations sufficiently explains Browning's intentions. Sir Charles Gavan Duffy, himself a Roman Catholic, recounts in his memoirs how Browning said, "Certainly I intended it for Cardinal Wiseman, but I don't consider it a satire, there is nothing hostile about it", and how Browning denied any antipathy to the Roman Church. Wiseman reviewed the poem in *The Rambler* in January 1856, and though he considered it might have a harmful effect, he was generous in his praise of its merits. In reading the poem it is necessary to bear in mind that it is in the form of a debate. Since it is a monologue we only hear the Bishop speak, but from what he says we can understand quite easily the points made on the other side. The word *Apology* in the title is not meant in the sense of *excuse*, but in the sense of *defence*, as Newman used its Latin equivalent in his *Apologia pro Vita sua.* But because it is a debate and because the Bishop's opponent, the young rationalist, Gigadibs, is his intellectual inferior, we are not given a full account of the fundamentals of the Bishop's faith. The end of the poem makes it clear that the Bishop has been arguing on ground chosen by Gigadibs and that the foundations of his own faith lie deeper than this. Browning tells us that "Blougram, he believed, say, half he spoke", and this cuts both ways. The Bishop's argument in one place rests on the case that he has made the best of both worlds, this one and the next. His faith promises immortality, but even if he is mistaken in this, he still enjoys power, acclaim, and wealth in this life. As for Gigadibs, his doubt promises nothing hereafter and gives him very little here. Why, then, should not Gigadibs make the gamble of faith rather than of doubt? This, of course, is a very cynical argument, but we do not know how far the Bishop accepts it for himself and how far he is using it as a tactic in debate to show the inconsistency of Gigadibs's position. But not all of the Bishop's arguments are as cynical as this. He can reach profound depths and sublime heights; his arguments at times, indeed, show a nobler belief than his own wordliness demonstrates. But this is true of many other believers; they would be the first to admit that their beliefs are better than themselves. One thing is manifest, however: if the Bishop's arguments are often sophistical and cynical, Gigadibs's rationalism is very shallow. The Bishop achieves his main purpose of showing Gigadibs how ill-founded is his lack of belief by throwing doubt on his doubt.

No more wine? Then we'll push back chairs and talk.
A final glass for me, though: cool, i'faith!
We ought to have our Abbey back, you see.
It's different, preaching in basilicas,
5 And doing duty in some masterpiece

3 *Abbey:* Westminster Abbey, which until the Reformation had belonged to the Roman Church.

4 *basilicas:* rectangular churches with an apsidal east end.

Like this of brother Pugin's, bless his heart!
I doubt if they're half baked, those chalk rosettes,
Ciphers and stucco-twiddlings everywhere;
It's just like breathing in a lime-kiln: eh?
10 These hot long ceremonies of our church
Cost us a little—oh, they pay the price,
You take me—amply pay it! Now, we'll talk.

So, you despise me, Mr. Gigadibs.
No deprecation,—nay, I beg you, sir!
15 Beside 'tis our engagement: don't you know,
I promised, if you'd watch a dinner out,
We'd see truth dawn together?—truth that peeps
Over the glass's edge when dinner's done,
And body gets its sop and holds its noise
20 And leaves soul free a little. Now's the time—
'Tis break of day! You do despise me then.
And if I say, "despise me,"—never fear—
I know you do not in a certain sense—
Not in my arm-chair for example: here,
25 I well imagine you respect my place
(Status, *entourage*, worldly circumstance)
Quite to its value—very much indeed
—Are up to the protesting eyes of you
In pride at being seated here for once—
30 You'll turn it to such capital account!
When somebody, through years and years to come,
Hints of the bishop,—names me—that's enough—
"Blougram? I knew him"—(into it you slide)
"Dined with him once, a Corpus Christi Day,
35 All alone, we two—he's a clever man—
And after dinner,—why, the wine you know,—

6 *Pugin:* A. W. N. Pugin (1812-52) was a convert to the Roman Church and was one of the leaders in the Victorian revival of Gothic. He designed many churches for the Roman Catholics. Most of the decoration of the House of Commons was designed by him. It is said that he and Cardinal Wiseman quarreled over church architecture.

Oh, there was wine, and good!—what with the wine . . .
'Faith, we began upon all sorts of talk!
He's no bad fellow, Blougram—he had seen
40 Something of mine he relished—some review—
He's quite above their humbug in his heart,
Half-said as much, indeed—the thing's his trade—
I warrant, Blougram's sceptical at times—
How otherwise? I liked him, I confess!"
45 *Che che*, my dear sir, as we say at Rome,
Don't you protest now! It's fair give and take;
You have had your turn and spoken your home-truths—
The hand's mine now, and here you follow suit.

Thus much conceded, still the first fact stays—
50 You do despise me; your ideal of life
Is not the bishop's—you would not be I—
You would like better to be Goethe, now,
Or Buonaparte—or, bless me, lower still,
Count D'Orsay,—so you did what you preferred,
55 Spoke as you thought, and, as you cannot help,
Believed or disbelieved, no matter what,
So long as on that point, whate'er it was,
You loosed your mind, were whole and sole yourself.
—That, my ideal never can include,
60 Upon that element of truth and worth
Never be based! for say they make me Pope
(They can't—suppose it for our argument)
Why, there I'm at my tether's end—I've reached
My height, and not a height which pleases you.
65 An unbelieving Pope won't do, you say.
It's like those eerie stories nurses tell,
Of how some actor played Death on a stage
With pasteboard crown, sham orb and tinselled dart,

45 *Che che:* What, what.

52 *Goethe:* the great German poet (1749-1832).

54 *Count D'Orsay:* (1798-1852) a leader of fashionable society in London and Paris.

And called himself the monarch of the world,
70 Then going in the tire-room afterward
Because the play was done, to shift himself,
Got touched upon the sleeve familiarly
The moment he had shut the closet door
By Death himself. Thus God might touch a Pope
75 At unawares, ask what his baubles mean,
And whose part he presumed to play just now?
Best be yourself, imperial, plain and true!

So, drawing comfortable breath again,
You weigh and find whatever more or less
80 I boast of my ideal realized
Is nothing in the balance when opposed
To your ideal, your grand simple life,
Of which you will not realize one jot.
I am much, you are nothing; you would be all,
85 I would be merely much—you beat me there.

No, friend, you do not beat me,—hearken why.
The common problem, yours, mine, every one's,
Is not to fancy what were fair in life
Provided it could be,—but, finding first
90 What may be, then find how to make it fair
Up to our means—a very different thing!
No abstract intellectual plan of life
Quite irrespective of life's plainest laws,
But one, a man, who is man and nothing more,
95 May lead within a world which (by your leave)
Is Rome or London—not Fool's-paradise.
Embellish Rome, idealize away,
Make Paradise of London if you can,
You're welcome, nay, you're wise.

A simile!
100 We mortals cross the ocean of this world
Each in his average cabin of a life—

The best's not big, the worst yields elbow-room.
Now for our six months' voyage—how prepare?
You come on shipboard with a landsman's list
105 Of things he calls convenient—so they are!
An India screen is pretty furniture,
A piano-forte is a fine resource,
All Balzac's novels occupy one shelf,
The new edition fifty volumes long;
110 And little Greek books, with the funny type
They get up well at Leipsic, fill the next—
Go on! slabbed marble, what a bath it makes!
And Parma's pride, the Jerome, let us add!
'Twere pleasant could Correggio's fleeting glow
115 Hang full in face of one where'er one roams,
Since he more than the others brings with him
Italy's self,--the marvellous Modenese!
Yet 'twas not on your list before, perhaps.
—Alas! friend, here's the agent . . . is't the name?
120 The captain, or whoever's master here—
You see him screw his face up; what's his cry
Ere you set foot on shipboard? "Six feet square!"
If you won't understand what six feet mean,
Compute and purchase stores accordingly—
125 And if in pique because he overhauls
Your Jerome, piano and bath, you come on board
Bare—why, you cut a figure at the first
While sympathetic landsmen see you off;
Not afterwards, when, long ere half seas over,
130 You peep up from your utterly naked boards
Into some snug and well-appointed berth,

108 *Balzac:* French novelist (1799-1850) whose work Browning admired. The references in this passage comprise music, literature, philosophy, and art.

113-14 *Parma . . . Correggio:* This refers to the famous painting of St. Jerome by Corregio (1494-1534) which hangs in Parma.

117 *Modenese:* Corregio was a native of Modena.

119 *agent:* i.e. the agent who acts for the ship's owners.

Like mine, for instance (try the cooler jug—
Put back the other, but don't jog the ice)
And mortified you mutter "Well and good—
135 He sits enjoying his sea-furniture—
'Tis stout and proper, and there's store of it,
Though I've the better notion, all agree,
Of fitting rooms up! hang the carpenter,
Neat ship-shape fixings and contrivances—
140 I would have brought my Jerome, frame and all!"
And meantime you bring nothing: never mind—
You've proved your artist-nature: what you don't,
You might bring, so despise me, as I say.

Now come, let's backward to the starting place.
145 See my way: we're two college friends, suppose—
Prepare together for our voyage, then,
Each note and check the other in his work,—
Here's mine, a bishop's outfit; criticize!
What's wrong? why won't you be a bishop too?

150 Why, first, you don't believe, you don't and can't,
(Not statedly, that is, and fixedly
And absolutely and exclusively)
In any revelation called divine.
No dogmas nail your faith—and what remains
155 But say so, like the honest man you are?
First, therefore, overhaul theology!
Nay, I too, not a fool, you please to think,
Must find believing every whit as hard,
And if I do not frankly say as much,
160 The ugly consequence is clear enough.

Now, wait, my friend: well, I do not believe—
If you'll accept no faith that is not fixed,
Absolute and exclusive, as you say.
(You're wrong—I mean to prove it in due time.)

160 *The ugly consequence:* i.e. the Bishop is a hypocrite.

165 Meanwhile, I know where difficulties lie
I could not, cannot solve, nor ever shall,
So give up hope accordingly to solve—
(To you, and over the wine). Our dogmas then
With both of us, though in unlike degree,
170 Missing full credence—overboard with them!
I mean to meet you on your own premise—
Good, there go mine in company with yours!

And now what are we? unbelievers both,
Calm and complete, determinately fixed
175 To-day, to-morrow, and for ever, pray?
You'll guarantee me that? Not so, I think!
In no-wise! all we've gained is, that belief,
As unbelief before, shakes us by fits,
Confounds us like its predecessor. Where's
180 The gain? how can we guard our unbelief,
Make it bear fruit to us?—the problem here.
Just when we are safest, there's a sunset-touch,
A fancy from a flower-bell, some one's death,
A chorus-ending from Euripides,—
185 And that's enough for fifty hopes and fears
As old and new at once as Nature's self,
To rap and knock and enter in our soul,
Take hands and dance there, a fantastic ring,
Round the ancient idol, on his base again,—
190 The grand Perhaps! we look on helplessly,—
There the old misgivings, crooked questions are—
This good God,—what He could do, if He would,
Would, if He could—then must have done long since:
If so, when, where, and how? some way must be,—
195 Once feel about, and soon or late you hit
Some sense, in which it might be, after all.
Why not, "The Way, the Truth, the Life?"

184 *Euripides:* Tragic dramatist of classical Greece (480-406 B.C.). In this passage the Bishop points out the difficulties not of belief but of unbelief. He invites Gigadibs to consider the possibility of the "grand Perhaps".

—That way
Over the mountain, which who stands upon
Is apt to doubt if it be indeed a road;
200 While if he views it from the waste itself,
Up goes the line there, plain from base to brow,
Not vague, mistakable! what's a break or two
Seen from the unbroken desert either side?
And then (to bring in fresh philosophy)
205 What if the breaks themselves should prove at last
The most consummate of contrivances
To train a man's eye, teach him what is faith,—
And so we stumble at truth's very test?
All we have gained then by our unbelief
210 Is a life of doubt diversified by faith,
For one of faith diversified by doubt:
We called the chess-board white,—we call it black.

"Well," you rejoin, "the end's no worse, at least
We've reason for both colours on the board.
215 Why not confess, then, where I drop the faith
And you the doubt, that I'm as right as you?"

Because, friend, in the next place, this being so,
And both things even,—faith and unbelief
Left to a man's choice,—we'll proceed a step,
220 Returning to our image, which I like.

A man's choice, yes—but a cabin-passenger's—
The man made for the special life of the world—
Do you forget him? I remember though!
Consult our ship's conditions and you find
225 One and but one choice suitable to all,
The choice, that you unluckily prefer,

220 *our image:* i.e. the image of the sea-voyage. The Bishop reminds his listener that these are not purely speculative matters, but of practical importance.

Turning things topsy-turvy—they or it
Going to the ground. Belief or unbelief
Bears upon life, determines its whole course,
230 Begins at its beginning. See the world
Such as it is,—you made it not, nor I;
I mean to take it as it is,—and you
Not so you'll take it,—though you get nought else.
I know the special kind of life I like,
235 What suits the most my idiosyncrasy,
Brings out the best of me and bears me fruit
In power, peace, pleasantness and length of days.
I find that positive belief does this
For me, and unbelief, no whit of this.
240 —For you, it does, however?—that we'll try!
'Tis clear, I cannot lead my life, at least,
Induce the world to let me peaceably,
Without declaring at the outset, "Friends,
I absolutely and peremptorily
245 Believe!"—I say faith is my waking life.
One sleeps, indeed, and dreams at intervals,
We know, but waking's the main point with us,
And my provision's for life's waking part.
Accordingly, I use heart, head and hands
250 All day, I build, scheme, study and make friends;
And when night overtakes me, down I lie,
Sleep, dream a little, and get done with it,
The sooner the better, to begin afresh.
What's midnight's doubt before the dayspring's faith?
255 You, the philosopher, that disbelieve,
That recognize the night, give dreams their weight—
To be consistent you should keep your bed,
Abstain from healthy acts that prove you a man,
For fear you drowse perhaps at unawares!
260 And certainly at night you'll sleep and dream,
Live through the day and bustle as you please.
And so you live to sleep as I to wake,
To unbelieve as I to still believe?

Well, and the common sense of the world calls you
265 Bed-ridden,—and its good things come to me.
Its estimation, which is half the fight,
That's the first cabin-comfort I secure—
The next . . . but you perceive with half an eye!
Come, come, it's best believing, if we may—
270 You can't but own that.

Next, concede again—
If once we choose belief, on all accounts
We can't be too decisive in our faith,
Conclusive and exclusive in its terms,
To suit the world which gives us the good things.
275 In every man's career are certain points
Whereon he dares not be indifferent;
The world detects him clearly, if he dares,
As baffled at the game, and losing life.
He may care little or he may care much
280 For riches, honour, pleasure, work, repose,
Since various theories of life and life's
Success are extant which might easily
Comport with either estimate of these;
And whoso chooses wealth or poverty,
285 Labour or quiet, is not judged a fool
Because his fellows would choose otherwise:
We let him choose upon his own account
So long as he's consistent with his choice.
But certain points, left wholly to himself,
290 When once a man has arbitrated on,
We say he must succeed there or go hang.
Thus, he should wed the woman he loves most
Or needs most, whatsoe'er the love or need—
For he can't wed twice. Then, he must avouch
295 Or follow, at the least, sufficiently,
The form of faith his conscience holds the best,
Whate'er the process of conviction was:
For nothing can compensate his mistake

On such a point, the man himself being judge—
300 He cannot wed twice, nor twice lose his soul.

Well now, there's one great form of Christian faith
I happened to be born in—which to teach
Was given me as I grew up, on all hands,
As best and readiest means of living by;
305 The same on examination being proved
The most pronounced moreover, fixed, precise
And absolute form of faith in the whole world—
Accordingly, most potent of all forms
For working on the world. Observe, my friend,
310 Such as you know me, I am free to say,
In these hard latter days which hamper one,
Myself, by no immoderate exercise
Of intellect and learning, and the tact
To let external forces work for me,
315 —Bid the street's stones be bread and they are bread,
Bid Peter's creed, or, rather, Hildebrand's,
Exalt me o'er my fellows in the world
And make my life an ease and joy and pride,
It does so,—which for me's a great point gained,
320 Who have a soul and body that exact
A comfortable care in many ways.
There's power in me and will to dominate
Which I must exercise, they hurt me else:
In many ways I need mankind's respect,
325 Obedience, and the love that's born of fear:
While at the same time, there's a taste I have,
A toy of soul, a titillating thing,
Refuses to digest these dainties crude.
The naked life is gross till clothed upon:
330 I must take what men offer, with a grace

316 *Peter's creed . . . Hildebrand's:* St. Peter, the Apostle, was the first Bishop of Rome, but Hildebrand, who took the title of Pope Gregory VII (1073-85), was the Pope who first established the temporal power of the Church and founded the medieval Papacy.

As though I would not, could I help it, take!
An uniform I wear though over-rich—
Something imposed on me, no choice of mine;
No fancy-dress worn for pure fancy's sake
335 And despicable therefore! now men kneel
And kiss my hand—of course the Church's hand.
Thus I am made, thus life is best for me,
And thus that it should be I have procured;
And thus it could not be another way,
340 I venture to imagine.

You'll reply—
So far my choice, no doubt, is a success;
But were I made of better elements,
With nobler instincts, purer tastes, like you,
I hardly would account the thing success
345 Though it do all for me I say.

But, friend,
We speak of what is—not of what might be,
And how 'twere better if 'twere otherwise.
I am the man you see here plain enough—
Grant I'm a beast, why beasts must lead beasts' lives!
350 Suppose I own at once to tail and claws—
The tailless man exceeds me; but being tailed
I'll lash out lion-fashion, and leave apes
To dock their stump and dress their haunches up.
My business is not to remake myself,
355 But make the absolute best of what God made.
Or—our first simile—though you proved me doomed
To a viler berth still, to the steerage-hole,
The sheep-pen or the pig-stye, I should strive
To make what use of each were possible;
360 And as this cabin gets upholstery,
That hutch should rustle with sufficient straw.

345 In the passage which follows Blougram maintains that even in the eyes of the world he has made a better job of things than Gigadibs.

But, friend, I don't acknowledge quite so fast
I fail of all your manhood's lofty tastes
Enumerated so complacently,
365 On the mere ground that you forsooth can find
In this particular life I choose to lead
No fit provision for them. Can you not?
Say you, my fault is I address myself
To grosser estimators than I need?
370 And that's no way of holding up the soul—
Which, nobler, needs men's praise perhaps, yet knows
One wise man's verdict outweighs all the fools',—
Would like the two, but, forced to choose, takes that?
I pine among my million imbeciles
375 (You think) aware some dozen men of sense
Eye me and know me, whether I believe
In the last winking Virgin, as I vow,
And am a fool, or disbelieve in her
And am a knave,—approve in neither case,
380 Withhold their voices though I look their way:
Like Verdi when, at his worst opera's end
(The thing they gave at Florence,—what's its name?)
While the mad houseful's plaudits near out-bang
His orchestra of salt-box, tongs and bones,
385 He looks through all the roaring and the wreaths
Where sits Rossini patient in his stall.
Nay, friend, I meet you with an answer here—
That even your prime men who appraise their kind
Are men still, catch a wheel within a wheel,
390 See more in a truth than the truth's simple self,

377 *the last winking Virgin:* statues of the Virgin which shed tears. Gigadibs would maintain that such things are impostures.

381 *Verdi:* Italian composer (1813-1901) whose early operas were failures. Blougram pictures the composer sitting at the conclusion of one of his later successful operas; the audience applauds, but Rossini, the expert, remains unmoved.

386 *Rossini:* a famous composer (1792-1868) of operas, such as *The Barber of Seville* and *William Tell.*

Confuse themselves. You see lads walk the street
Sixty the minute; what's to note in that?
You see one lad o'erstride a chimney-stack;
Him you must watch—he's sure to fall, yet stands!
395 Our interest's on the dangerous edge of things.
The honest thief, the tender murderer,
The superstitious atheist, demireps
That love and save their souls in new French books—
We watch while these in equilibrium keep
400 The giddy line midway: one step aside,
They're classed and done with. I, then, keep the line
Before your sages,—just the men to shrink
From the gross weights, coarse scales, and labels broad
You offer their refinement. Fool or knave?
405 Why needs a bishop be a fool or knave
When there's a thousand diamond weights between?
So I enlist them. Your picked Twelve, you'll find,
Profess themselves indignant, scandalized
At thus being held unable to explain
410 How a superior man who disbelieves
May not believe as well: that's Schelling's way!
It's through my coming in the tail of time,
Nicking the minute with a happy tact.
Had I been born three hundred years ago
415 They'd say, "What's strange? Blougram of course believes;"
And, seventy years since, "disbelieves of course".
But now, "He may believe; and yet, and yet
How can he?"—All eyes turn with interest.
Whereas, step off the line on either side—
420 You, for example, clever to a fault,
The rough and ready man that write apace,

397 *demireps:* women of doubtful reputation.

407 *Your picked Twelve:* i.e. any jury Gigadibs likes to choose would give Blougram the benefit of the doubt.

411 *Schelling:* German philosopher (1775-1854) of the Idealist school. Coleridge's philosophy was akin to Schelling's. On Schelling's view, any truth was only an approximation to the Absolute.

Read somewhat seldomer, think perhaps even less—
You disbelieve! Who wonders and who cares?
Lord So-and-So—his coat bedropt with wax,
425 All Peter's chains about his waist, his back
Brave with the needlework of Noodledom,
Believes! Again, who wonders and who cares?
But I, the man of sense and learning too,
The able to think yet act, the this, the that,
430 I, to believe at this late time of day!
Enough; you see, I need not fear contempt.

—Except it's yours! admire me as these may,
You don't. But whom at least do you admire?
Present your own perfections, your ideal,
435 Your pattern man for a minute—oh, make haste!
Is it Napoleon you would have us grow?
Concede the means; allow his head and hand,
(A large concession, clever as you are)
Good!—In our common primal element
440 Of unbelief (we can't believe, you know—
We're still at that admission, recollect)—
Where do you find—apart from, towering o'er
The secondary temporary aims
Which satisfy the gross tastes you despise—
445 Where do you find his star?—his crazy trust
God knows through what or in what? it's alive
And shines and leads him and that's all we want.
Have we aught in our sober night shall point
Such ends as his were, and direct the means
450 Of working out our purpose straight as his,
Nor bring a moment's trouble on success

424-7 Blougram implies that Gigadibs's unbelief is just as naïve as the belief of, say a pious Catholic nobleman whose coat is covered with the wax of his devotional candles, who wears chains (for cross and rosary) as massive as those St. Peter wore in prison, and whose vestments are embroidered by foolish women.

432 In the lines which follow Blougram argues that all great men, all who accomplish something, have some kind of faith.

With after-care to justify the same?
—Be a Napoleon and yet disbelieve!
Why, the man's mad, friend, take his light away.
455 What's the vague good of the world for which you'd dare
With comfort to yourself blow millions up?
We neither of us see it! we do see
The blown-up millions—spatter of their brains
And writhing of their bowels and so forth
460 In that bewildering entanglement
Of horrible eventualities
Past calculation to the end of time!
Can I mistake for some clear word of God
(Which were my ample warrant for it all)
465 His puff of hazy instincts, idle talk,
"The State, that's I," quack-nonsense about crowns,
And (when one beats the man to his last hold)
The vague idea of setting things to rights,
Policing people efficaciously,
470 More to their profit, most of all to his own;
The whole to end that dismallest of ends
By an Austrian marriage, cant to us the church,
And resurrection of the old *régime*.
Would I, who hope to live a dozen years,
475 Fight Austerlitz for reasons such and such?
No: for, concede me but the merest chance
Doubt may be wrong—there's judgment, life to come!
With just that chance, I dare not. Doubt proves right?
This present life is all?—you offer me
480 Its dozen noisy years without a chance

454 *take his light away:* i.e. in case he sets the place on fire.

466 "*The State, that's I*"*:* The principle of absolute sovereignty was first expressed in the phrase "L'état, c'est moi!" by Louis XIV of France.

472–3 *Austrian marriage . . . old* régime: Napoleon tried to stabilize his rule by allying himself to the old *régime*, and so married Marie-Louise, daughter of the Austrian Emperor, after the battle of Austerlitz.

475 *Austerlitz:* Napoleon defeated the forces of Austria, Russia and England at Austerlitz in 1805.

That wedding an Arch-Duchess, wearing lace,
And getting called by divers new-coined names,
Will drive off ugly thoughts and let me dine,
Sleep, read and chat in quiet as I like!
Therefore, I will not.

485 Take another case;
Fit up the cabin yet another way.
What say you to the poets? shall we write
Hamlets, Othellos—make the world our own,
Without a risk to run of either sort?
490 I can't!—to put the strongest reason first.
"But try," you urge, "the trying shall suffice:
The aim, if reached or not, makes great the life.
Try to be Shakspeare, leave the rest to fate!"
Spare my self-knowledge—there's no fooling me!
495 If I prefer remaining my poor self,
I say so not in self-dispraise but praise.
If I'm a Shakspeare, let the well alone—
Why should I try to be what now I am?
If I'm no Shakspeare, as too probable,—
500 His power and consciousness and self-delight
And all we want in common, shall I find—
Trying for ever? while on points of taste
Wherewith, to speak it humbly, he and I
Are dowered alike—I'll ask you, I or he,
505 Which in our two lives realizes most?
Much, he imagined—somewhat, I possess.
He had the imagination; stick to that!
Let him say "In the face of my soul's works
Your world is worthless and I touch it not
510 Lest I should wrong them"—I'll withdraw my plea.
But does he say so? look upon his life!
Himself, who only can, gives judgment there.
He leaves his towers and gorgeous palaces

513 *towers and gorgeous palaces:* a reference to Prospero's speech in *The Tempest*, IV, 1, 151, "And, like the baseless fabric of this vision,/The cloud-capped towers, the gorgeous palaces," etc.

To build the trimmest house in Stratford town:
515 Saves money, spends it, owns the worth of things,
Giulio Romano's pictures, Dowland's lute;
Enjoys a show, respects the puppets, too,
And none more, had he seen its entry once,
Than "Pandulph, of fair Milan cardinal."
520 Why then should I who play that personage,
The very Pandulph Shakspeare's fancy made,
Be told that had the poet chanced to start
From where I stand now (some degree like mine
Being just the goal he ran his race to reach)
525 He would have run the whole race back, forsooth,
And left being Pandulph, to begin write plays?
Ah, the earth's best can be but the earth's best!
Did Shakspeare live, he could but sit at home
And get himself in dreams the Vatican,
530 Greek busts, Venetian paintings, Roman walls,
And English books, none equal to his own,
Which I read, bound in gold, (he never did).
—Terni and Naples' bay and Gothard's top—
Eh, friend? I could not fancy one of these—
535 But, as I pour this claret, there they are—
I've gained them—crossed St. Gothard last July
With ten mules to the carriage and a bed

514 *the trimmest house:* On retiring from the London theatre Shakespeare bought New Place, reputed to be the most splendid house in Stratford upon-Avon.

516 *Giulio Romano:* a sixteenth-century Italian painter. We can see that Shakespeare knew his work from a reference to him in *The Winter's Tale* (V, ii, 90), "A piece [the statue of Hermione] many years in doing, and now newly performed by that rare Italian master, Julio Romano. . . ." *Dowland:* John Dowland (1563-1626) was a famous lutanist and composer of songs and airs.

519 *Pandulph:* a thirteenth-century cardinal who figures as the Papal legate to the king in Shakespeare's *King John* (III, i, 138).

533 *Terni:* the scene of some famous water-falls, forty miles from Rome. *Gothard's top* refers to the famous pass of St. Gothard in the Alps.

Slung inside; is my hap the worse for that?
We want the same things, Shakspeare and myself,
540 And what I want, I have: he, gifted more,
Could fancy he too had it when he liked,
But not so thoroughly that if fate allowed
He would not have it also in my sense.
We play one game. I send the ball aloft
545 No less adroitly that of fifty strokes
Scarce five go o'er the wall so wide and high
Which sends them back to me: I wish and get.
He struck balls higher and with better skill,
But at a poor fence level with his head,
550 And hit—his Stratford house, a coat of arms,
Successful dealings in his grain and wool,—
While I receive heaven's incense in my nose
And style myself the cousin of Queen Bess.
Ask him, if this life's all, who wins the game?

555 Believe—and our whole argument breaks up.
Enthusiasm's the best thing, I repeat;
Only, we can't command it; fire and life
Are all, dead matter's nothing, we agree:
And be it a mad dream or God's very breath,
560 The fact's the same,—belief's fire once in us,
Makes of all else mere stuff to show itself.
We penetrate our life with such a glow
As fire lends wood and iron—this turns steel,
That burns to ash—all's one, fire proves its power
565 For good or ill, since men call flare success.
But paint a fire, it will not therefore burn.
Light one in me, I'll find it food enough!
Why, to be Luther—that's a life to lead,
Incomparably better than my own.
570 He comes, reclaims God's earth for God, he says,

553 *cousin of Queen Bess:* The sovereign is Head of the Church of England, and since Blougram is Head of the Roman Church in England, they can be regarded as cousins.

Sets up God's rule again by simple means,
Re-opens a shut book, and all is done.
He flared out in the flaring of mankind;
Such Luther's luck was—how shall such be mine?
575 If he succeeded, nothing's left to do:
And if he did not altogether—well,
Strauss is the next advance. All Strauss should be
I might be also. But to what result?
He looks upon no future: Luther did.
580 What can I gain on the denying side?
Ice makes no conflagration. State the facts,
Read the text right, emancipate the world—
The emancipated world enjoys itself
With scarce a thank-you—Blougram told it first
585 It could not owe a farthing,—not to him
More than St. Paul! 'twould press its pay, you think?
Then add there's still that plaguy hundredth chance
Strauss may be wrong. And so a risk is run—
For what gain? not for Luther's, who secured
590 A real Heaven in his heart throughout his life,
Supposing death a little altered things!

"Ay, but since really you lack faith," you cry,
"You run the same risk really on all sides,
In cool indifference as bold unbelief.
595 As well be Strauss as swing 'twixt Paul and him.
It's not worth having, such imperfect faith,
Nor more available to do faith's work
Than unbelief like mine. Whole faith, or none!"

577 *Strauss:* German Biblical Scholar (1808-74); see Introduction, p. 10. Blougram contrasts the enthusiasm of Luther with the negative result of Strauss's influence.

585 *It could not owe a farthing:* Strauss emancipates people from the obligation of belief and gets no reward, not even a "thank-you"; Blougram with the authority of the Church exacts the utmost farthing of acknowledgment from his followers.

591 *Supposing death . . . altered things!:* Blougram means that Luther, as a heretic, will risk damnation after death.

Softly, my friend! I must dispute that point.
600 Once own the use of faith, I'll find you faith.
We're back on Christian ground. You call for faith;
I show you doubt, to prove that faith exists.
The more of doubt, the stronger faith, I say,
If faith o'ercomes doubt. How I know it does?
605 By life and man's free will, God gave for that!
To mould life as we choose it, shows our choice:
That's our one act, the previous work's His own.
You criticize the soil? it reared this tree—
This broad life and whatever fruit it bears!
610 What matter though I doubt at every pore,
Head-doubts, heart-doubts, doubts at my fingers' ends,
Doubts in the trivial work of every day,
Doubts at the very bases of my soul
In the grand moments when she probes herself—
615 If finally I have a life to show,
The thing I did, brought out in evidence
Against the thing done to me underground
By Hell and all its brood, for aught I know?
I say, whence sprang this? shows it faith or doubt?
620 All's doubt in me; where's break of faith in this?
It is the idea, the feeling and the love
God means mankind should strive for and show forth,
Whatever be the process to that end,—

599 ff. In the following lines the Bishop reaches the core of his argument. He admits and even insists that doubt must accompany faith, but once allow faith at all, "We're back on Christian ground" (599-646). Absolute faith is impossible for this would be knowledge and not faith. Faith has to be kept alive by the challenge of doubt (647-75). Even in the Middle Ages when faith was strong, the sanctions of reward and punishment after death were not sufficient to maintain moral conduct (676-92). Blougram argues that if faith is to be worthy of its name it must accept apparent impossibilities, and he is not ready to abandon a single miracle (693-746).

617 *the thing done to me underground:* Blougram has been arguing that faith is a matter of the will, of commitment, and this is what counts, not the unconscious or subconscious emotions that are possibly the work of devils.

And not historic knowledge, logic sound,
625 And metaphysical acumen, sure!
"What think ye of Christ," friend? when all's done and said,
You like this Christianity or not?
It may be false, but will you wish it true?
Has it your vote to be so if it can?
630 Trust you an instinct silenced long ago
That will break silence and enjoin you love
What mortified philosophy is hoarse,
And all in vain, with bidding you despise?
If you desire faith—then you've faith enough:
635 What else seeks God—nay, what else seek ourselves?
You form a notion of me, we'll suppose,
On hearsay; it's a favourable one:
"But still" (you add), "there was no such good man,
Because of contradictions in the facts.
640 One proves, for instance, he was born in Rome,
This Blougram—yet throughout the tales of him
I see he figures as an Englishman."
Well, the two things are reconcilable.
But would I rather you discovered that,
645 Subjoining—"Still, what matter though they be?
Blougram concerns me nought, born here or there."

Pure faith indeed—you know not what you ask!
Naked belief in God the Omnipotent,
Omniscient, Omnipresent, sears too much
650 The sense of conscious creatures to be borne.
It were the seeing Him, no flesh shall dare.
Some think, Creation's meant to show Him forth:
I say, it's meant to hide Him all it can,
And that's what all the blessed Evil's for.

644 *But would I rather:* i.e. Blougram would prefer Gigadibs to be interested in him, in spite of contradictory stories about his birth, than to ignore him. Wiseman, although English, was born in Seville.

654 *blessed Evil:* Evil has a place in the divine dispensation as a challenge to man's faith.

655 Its use in Time is to environ us,
Our breath, our drop of dew, with shield enough
Against that sight till we can bear its stress.
Under a vertical sun, the exposed brain
And lidless eye and disemprisoned heart
660 Less certainly would wither up at once
Than mind, confronted with the truth of Him.
But time and earth case-harden us to live;
The feeblest sense is trusted most; the child
Feels God a moment, ichors o'er the place,
665 Plays on and grows to be a man like us.
With me, faith means perpetual unbelief
Kept quiet like the snake 'neath Michael's foot
Who stands calm just because he feels it writhe.
Or, if that's too ambitious,—here's my box—
670 I need the excitation of a pinch
Threatening the torpor of the inside-nose
Nigh on the imminent sneeze that never comes.
"Leave it in peace" advise the simple folk—
Make it aware of peace by itching-fits,
675 Say I—let doubt occasion still more faith!

You'll say, once all believed, man, woman, child,
In that dear middle-age these noodles praise.
How you'd exult if I could put you back
Six hundred years, blot out cosmogony,
680 Geology, ethnology, what not,
(Greek endings with the little passing-bell
That signifies some faith's about to die)
And set you square with Genesis again,—
When such a traveller told you his last news,
685 He saw the ark a-top of Ararat

664 *ichors o'er the place:* The innocent vision of the child is covered over just as a wound heals over by the discharge of fluid (ichor).

667 *Michael's foot:* St. Michael is generally depicted as trampling on the dragon. A good modern example is Epstein's sculpture on the exterior of the new Coventry Cathedral.

But did not climb there since 'twas getting dusk
And robber-bands infest the mountain's foot!
How should you feel, I ask, in such an age,
How act? As other people felt and did;
690 With soul more blank than this decanter's knob,
Believe—and yet lie, kill, rob, fornicate
Full in belief's face, like the beast you'd be!

No, when the fight begins within himself,
A man's worth something. God stoops o'er his head,
695 Satan looks up between his feet—both tug—
He's left, himself, in the middle: the soul wakes
And grows. Prolong that battle through his life!
Never leave growing till the life to come!
Here, we've got callous to the Virgin's winks
700 That used to puzzle people wholesomely—
Men have outgrown the shame of being fools.
What are the laws of Nature, not to bend
If the Church bid them?—brother Newman asks.
Up with the Immaculate Conception, then—
705 On to the rack with faith!—is my advice.
Will not that hurry us upon our knees
Knocking our breasts, "It can't be—yet it shall!
Who am I, the worm, to argue with my Pope?
Low things confound the high things!" and so forth.
710 That's better than acquitting God with grace
As some folks do. He's tried—no case is proved,
Philosophy is lenient—He may go!

703 *I, the Church bid them?:* For the believer, the Church has the power to work miracles, that is, to suspend or bend the laws of Nature. *Newman:* John Henry Newman, leader of the Tractarians, was a convert to Rome and was finally made a Cardinal. In his *Lectures on the Present Position of Catholics in England*, Newman argued for the credibility of miracles.

704 *Immaculate Conception:* the dogma that the Virgin Mary was born free of original sin. After great controversy this became a dogma of the Roman Catholic Church in 1854.

You'll say—the old system's not so obsolete
But men believe still: ay, but who and where?
715 King Bomba's lazzaroni foster yet
The sacred flame, so Antonelli writes;
But even of these, what ragamuffin-saint
Believes God watches him continually,
As he believes in fire that it will burn,
720 Or rain that it will drench him? Break fire's law,
Sin against rain, although the penalty
Be just a singe or soaking? No, he smiles;
Those laws are laws that can enforce themselves.

The sum of all is—yes, my doubt is great,
725 My faith's still greater—then my faith's enough.
I have read much, thought much, experienced much,
Yet would die rather than avow my fear
The Naples' liquefaction may be false,
When set to happen by the palace-clock
730 According to the clouds or dinner-time.
I hear you recommend, I might at least
Eliminate, decrassify my faith
Since I adopt it; keeping what I must
And leaving what I can—such points as this!
735 I won't—that is, I can't throw one away.
Supposing there's no truth in what I said
About the need of trials to man's faith,
Still, when you bid me purify the same,
To such a process I discern no end,

715 *King Bomba:* a nickname given to Ferdinand II (1830–59), King of the two Sicilies, and meaning "bombastic" or "braggart". *lazzaroni:* a name given to beggars in Italy.

716 *Antonelli:* Cardinal Antonelli was secretary to Pope Pius IX.

728 *Naples' liquefaction:* Some congealed blood of St. Januarius (a fourth-century martyr) is kept in the cathedral at Naples and is said to liquefy each year on the saint's feast-day in September. Newman had defended belief in this phenomenon in his *Lectures* (see note on 703).

732 *decrassify:* divest of what is gross or material.

740 Clearing off one excrescence to see two;
There's ever a next in size, now grown as big,
That meets the knife—I cut and cut again!
First cut the Liquefaction, what comes last
But Fichte's clever cut at God himself?
745 Experimentalize on sacred things?
I trust nor hand nor eye nor heart nor brain
To stop betimes: they all get drunk alike.
The first step, I am master not to take.

You'd find the cutting-process to your taste
750 As much as leaving growths of lies unpruned,
Nor see more danger in it, you retort.
Your taste's worth mine; but my taste proves more wise
When we consider that the steadfast hold
On the extreme end of the chain of faith
755 Gives all the advantage, makes the difference,
With the rough purblind mass we seek to rule.
We are their lords, or they are free of us
Just as we tighten or relax that hold.
So, other matters equal, we'll revert
760 To the first problem—which, if solved my way
And thrown into the balance, turns the scale—
How we may lead a comfortable life,
How suit our luggage to the cabin's size.

Of course you are remarking all this time
765 How narrowly and grossly I view life,
Respect the creature-comforts, care to rule

744 *Fichte:* J. G. Fichte (1762–1814), a German, idealist philosopher, who argued that God is a universal self made up of all the individual selves of mankind, that is, a universal soul in which we all partake.

764 Blougram now turns to that part of his argument which accuses Gigadibs of inconsistency in not following his own disbelief to its logical and practical conclusion. Gigadibs, maintains the Bishop, is more of a hypocrite than himself, for he (the Bishop) makes more of this world than his materialist opponent.

The masses, and regard complacently
"The cabin," in our old phrase! Well, I do.
I act for, talk for, live for this world now,
770 As this world calls for action, life and talk—
No prejudice to what next world may prove,
Whose new laws and requirements, my best pledge
To observe then, is that I observe these now,
Shall do hereafter what I do meanwhile.
775 Let us concede (gratuitously though)
Next life relieves the soul of body, yields
Pure spiritual enjoyments: well, my friend,
Why lose this life in the meantime, since its use
May be to make the next life more intense?

780 Do you know, I have often had a dream
(Work it up in your next month's article)
Of man's poor spirit in its progress still
Losing true life for ever and a day
Through ever trying to be and ever being
785 In the evolution of successive spheres,
Before its actual sphere and place of life,
Halfway into the next, which having reached,
It shoots with corresponding foolery
Halfway into the next still, on and off!
790 As when a traveller, bound from North to South,
Scouts fur in Russia—what's its use in France?
In France spurns flannel—where's its need in Spain?
In Spain drops cloth—too cumbrous for Algiers!
Linen goes next, and last the skin itself,
795 A superfluity at Timbuctoo.
When, through his journey, was the fool at ease?
I'm at ease now, friend—worldly in this world
I take and like its way of life; I think
My brothers who administer the means
800 Live better for my comfort—that's good too;
And God, if He pronounce upon it all,
Approves my service, which is better still.

If He keep silence,—why, for you or me
Or that brute-beast pulled-up in to-day's "Times,"
805 What odds is't, save to ourselves, what life we lead?

You meet me at this issue—you declare,
All special pleading done with, truth is truth,
And justifies itself by undreamed ways.
You don't fear but it's better, if we doubt,
810 To say so, acting up to our truth perceived
However feebly. Do then,—act away!
'Tis there I'm on the watch for you! How one acts
Is, both of us agree, our chief concern:
And how you'll act is what I fain would see
815 If, like the candid person you appear,
You dare to make the most of your life's scheme
As I of mine, live up to its full law
Since there's no higher law that counterchecks.
Put natural religion to the test
820 You've just demolished the revealed with—quick,
Down to the root of all that checks your will,
All prohibition to lie, kill, and thieve
Or even to be an atheistic priest!
Suppose a pricking to incontinence—
825 Philosophers deduce you chastity
Or shame, from just the fact that at the first
Whoso embraced a woman in the plain,
Threw club down, and forewent his brains beside,
So stood a ready victim in the reach
830 Of any brother-savage club in hand—
Hence saw the use of going out of sight
In wood or cave to prosecute his loves—
I read this in a French book t'other day.
Does law so analyzed coerce you much?
835 Oh, men spin clouds of fuzz where matters end,
But you who reach where the first thread begins,

825 In the following lines Blougram scoffs at the popular Victorian notion that morals can be deduced from Nature.

You'll soon cut that!—which means you can, but won't
Through certain instincts, blind, unreasoned-out,
You dare not set aside, you can't tell why,
840 But there they are, and so you let them rule.
Then, friend, you seem as much a slave as I,
A liar, conscious coward and hypocrite,
Without the good the slave expects to get,
Suppose he has a master after all!
845 You own your instincts—why, what else do I,
Who want, am made for, and must have a God
Ere I can be aught, do aught?—no mere name
Want, but the true thing with what proves its truth,
To wit, a relation from that thing to me,
850 Touching from head to foot—which touch I feel,
And with it take the rest, this life of ours!
I live my life here; yours you dare not live.

—Not as I state it, who (you please subjoin)
Disfigure such a life and call it names,
855 While, in your mind, remains another way
For simple men: knowledge and power have rights,
But ignorance and weakness have rights too.
There needs no crucial effort to find truth
If here or there or anywhere about—
860 We ought to turn each side, try hard and see,
And if we can't, be glad we've earned at least
The right, by one laborious proof the more,
To graze in peace earth's pleasant pasturage.
Men are not angels, neither are they brutes.
865 Something we may see, all we cannot see—
What need of lying? I say, I see all,
And swear to each detail the most minute
In what I think a Pan's face—you, mere cloud:
I swear I hear him speak and see him wink,
870 For fear, if once I drop the emphasis,
Mankind may doubt there's any cloud at all.
You take the simpler life—ready to see,

Willing to see—for no cloud's worth a face—
And leaving quiet what no strength can move,
875 And which, who bids you move? who has the right?
I bid you; but you are God's sheep, not mine—
"*Pastor est tui Dominus.*" You find
In these the pleasant pastures of this life
Much you may eat without the least offence,
880 Much you don't eat because your maw objects,
Much you would eat but that your fellow-flock
Open great eyes at you and even butt,
And thereupon you like your mates so well
You cannot please yourself, offending them—
885 Though when they seem exorbitantly sheep,
You weigh your pleasure with their butts and bleats
And strike the balance. Sometimes certain fears
Restrain you—real checks since you find them so—
Sometimes you please yourself and nothing checks;
890 And thus you graze through life with not one lie,
And like it best.

But do you, in truth's name?
If so, you beat—which means, you are not I—
Who needs must make earth mine and feed my fill
Not simply unbutted at, unbickered with,
895 But motioned to the velvet of the sward
By those obsequious wethers' very selves.
Look at me, sir; my age is double yours:
At yours, I knew beforehand, so enjoyed,
What now I should be—as, permit the word,
900 I pretty well imagine your whole range
And stretch of tether twenty years to come.
We both have minds and bodies much alike.
In truth's name, don't you want my bishopric,

877 "*Pastor est tui Dominus*"*:* The Lord is thy Shepherd—a reference to *Psalm* XXIII, which begins "The Lord is my Shepherd".

892 *beat:* This intransitive use of the verb still survives in nautical terminology; e.g. a ship beats into the wind or against the current.

My daily bread, my influence and my state?
905 You're young, I'm old, you must be old one day;
Will you find then, as I do hour by hour,
Women their lovers kneel to, that cut curls
From your fat lap-dog's ears to grace a brooch—
Dukes, that petition just to kiss your ring—
910 With much beside you know or may conceive?
Suppose we die to-night: well, here am I,
Such were my gains, life bore this fruit to me,
While writing all the same my articles
On music, poetry, the fictile vase
915 Found at Albano, chess, or Anacreon's Greek.
But you—the highest honour in your life,
The thing you'll crown yourself with, all your days,
Is—dining here and drinking this last glass
I pour you out in sign of amity
920 Before we part for ever. Of your power
And social influence, worldly worth in short,
Judge what's my estimation by the fact,
I do not condescend to enjoin, beseech,
Hint secrecy on one of all these words!
925 You're shrewd and know that should you publish one
The world would brand the lie—my enemies first,
Who'd sneer—"The bishop's an arch-hypocrite,
And knave perhaps, but not so frank a fool."
Whereas I should not dare for both my ears
930 Breathe one such syllable, smile one such smile,
Before my chaplain who reflects myself—
My shade's so much more potent than your flesh.
What's your reward, self-abnegating friend?
Stood you confessed of those exceptional
935 And privileged great natures that dwarf mine—

914 The following lines indicate the Bishop's virtuosity. Wiseman in fact was a learned and prolific writer on the arts and religion. "Fictile" means plastic, and the reference is to Blougram's knowledge of ceramics. Albano is a village outside Rome. Anacreon was a Greek lyric poet of the 6th century B.C.

A zealot with a mad ideal in reach,
A poet just about to print his ode,
A statesman with a scheme to stop this war,
An artist whose religion is his art,
940 I should have nothing to object! such men
Carry the fire, all things grow warm to them,
Their drugget's worth my purple, they beat me.
But you,—you're just as little those as I—
You, Gigadibs, who, thirty years of age,
945 Write statedly for Blackwood's Magazine,
Believe you see two points in Hamlet's soul
Unseized by the Germans yet—which view you'll print—
Meantime the best you have to show being still
That lively lightsome article we took
950 Almost for the true Dickens,—what's its name?
"The Slum and Cellar—or Whitechapel life
Limned after dark!" it made me laugh, I know,
And pleased a month and brought you in ten pounds.
—Success I recognize and compliment,
955 And therefore give you, if you please, three words
(The card and pencil-scratch is quite enough)
Which whether here, in Dublin or New York,
Will get you, prompt as at my eyebrow's wink,
Such terms as never you aspired to get
960 In all our own reviews and some not ours.
Go write your lively sketches—be the first
"Blougram, or The Eccentric Confidence"—
Or better simply say, "The Outward-bound."
Why, men as soon would throw it in my teeth
965 As copy and quote the infamy chalked broad
About me on the church-door opposite.
You will not wait for that experience though,
I fancy, howsoever you decide,

942 *drugget:* a coarse cheap cloth.

945 *Blackwood's Magazine:* an influential periodical.

957 *in Dublin:* Wiseman was one of the founders of the *Dublin Review* in 1836.

To discontinue—not detesting, not
970 Defaming, but at least—despising me!

Over his wine so smiled and talked his hour
Sylvester Blougram, styled *in partibus*
Episcopus, nec non—(the deuce knows what
It's changed to by our novel hierarchy)
975 With Gigadibs the literary man,
Who played with spoons, explored his plate's design,
And ranged the olive stones about its edge,
While the great bishop rolled him out his mind.

For Blougram, he believed, say, half he spoke.
980 The other portion, as he shaped it thus
For argumentatory purposes,
He felt his foe was foolish to dispute.
Some arbitrary accidental thoughts
That crossed his mind, amusing because new,
985 He chose to represent as fixtures there,
Invariable convictions (such they seemed
Beside his interlocutor's loose cards
Flung daily down, and not the same way twice)
While certain Hell-deep instincts, man's weak tongue
990 Is never bold to utter in their truth
Because styled Hell-deep ('tis an old mistake
To place Hell at the bottom of the earth)
He ignored these,—not having in readiness
Their nomenclature and philosophy:
995 He said true things, but called them by wrong names.
"On the whole," he thought, "I justify myself
On every point where cavillers like this

972–3 *in partibus Episcopus:* a reference to Wiseman's change of title. Before 1850 Wiseman was Bishop of Melipotamus *in partibus infidelium* (in regions of the unfaithful); that is, he took his title from some other see, but was Head of the Roman Catholics in England. In 1850 the Roman hierarchy was re-established in England and he became Archbishop of Westminster.

Oppugn my life: he tries one kind of fence—
I close—he's worsted, that's enough for him;
1000 He's on the ground! if the ground should break away
I take my stand on, there's a firmer yet
Beneath it, both of us may sink and reach.
His ground was over mine and broke the first.
So let him sit with me this many a year!"

1005 He did not sit five minutes. Just a week
Sufficed his sudden healthy vehemence.
(Something had struck him in the "Outward-bound"
Another way than Blougram's purpose was)
And having bought, not cabin-furniture
1010 But settler's-implements (enough for three)
And started for Australia—there, I hope,
By this time he has tested his first plough,
And studied his last chapter of St. John.

1013 *his last chapter of St. John:* At the conclusion of the poem Gigadibs is left in a state of doubt about his doubts. He gives up journalism and emigrates to Australia where, the poet hopes, he will study the Gospels, especially the concluding chapter of St. John's Gospel in which the risen Jesus appears to the disciples.

PROSPICE

THIS poem was written after the death of the poet's wife in 1861, and was published in *Dramatis Personae*, 1864. The title means "Look forward", and the poem is a fearless confrontation with the thought of death. The death of his wife was a terrible blow to Browning, and for several years after it he shunned society and led the life of a recluse. Many writers have accused Browning of an easy optimism, but his life makes it clear that he knew periods of despair and *angst*. He said, after his wife's death, that he felt they had both been walking across a torrent on a straw. This poem expresses defiance and courage in the face of death, but Browning had won through to this confidence only after intense spiritual and emotional turmoil.

Fear death?—to feel the fog in my throat,
  The mist in my face,
When the snows begin, and the blasts denote
  I am nearing the place,
5 The power of the night the press of the storm,
  The post of the foe;
Where he stands, the Arch Fear in a visible form;
  Yet the strong man must go:
  For the journey is done and the summit attained,
10 And the barriers fall,
Though a battle's to fight ere the guerdon be gained,
  The reward of it all.
I was ever a fighter so—one fight more,
  The best and the last!
15 I would hate that death bandaged my eyes, and forbore,
  And bade me creep past.
No! let me taste the whole of it, fare like my peers
  The heroes of old,
Bear the brunt, in a minute pay glad life's arrears
20 Of pain, darkness and cold.
For sudden the worst turns the best to the brave,
  The black minute's at end,
And the elements' rage, the fiend-voices that rave,
  Shall dwindle, shall blend,
25 Shall change, shall become first a peace, then a joy,
  Then a light, then thy breast,
O thou soul of my soul! I shall clasp thee again,
  And with God be the rest!

27 *soul of my soul:* i.e. the poet's wife.

Dante Gabriel Rossetti

FOR
OUR LADY OF THE ROCKS
BY LEONARDO DA VINCI

D. G. ROSSETTI was an accomplished painter as well as a poet. He was born in London, but his father was Italian and his mother half Italian. The father was a professor at King's College, London, and a life-long student of Dante, and Rossetti himself was inspired by Dante. In 1848 Rossetti joined Holman Hunt and Millais in forming the Pre-Raphaelite Brotherhood, the main purpose of which was to recapture the vision and freshness of the great period of Italian painting that culminated in Raphael (1483-1520). Their conception of what they regarded as the great age of Christian faith was rather vague, and the movement they initiated was largely an aesthetic one without any doctrinal foundations. Today, we see this group, and the men who gathered around them, as heirs of the Romantic Revival and rebels against the vulgarisation of Victorian taste that accompanied the industrial revolution. One of Dante's themes that Rossetti made his own was the approximation of human to divine love, of physical to spiritual beauty. Coupled with this was an idealisation of woman and a veneration for the Virgin Mary. But with all his regard for spiritualised love, Rossetti had a vivid appreciation of sensuous beauty and it is the fusion of the two which gives his paintings and poetry their most characteristic quality. The poem that follows is one of a series of sonnets which Rossetti wrote on certain famous paintings, and was inspired by *Our Lady of the Rocks*, by Leonardo da Vinci (1452-1519), which hangs in the National Gallery. In this painting the Virgin is depicted as *Mater Dolorosa*, the mother of sorrows, who grieves not only for the sufferings that await her Son, but for the sufferings of mankind. In spite of this and of her mysterious and sombre surroundings, Leonardo's genius endows his central figure with a serenity and an air of victory that transcend her sadness.

Mother, is this the darkness of the end,
  The Shadow of Death? and is that outer sea
  Infinite imminent Eternity?
And does the death-pang by man's seed sustained
5 In Time's each instant cause thy face to bend
  Its silent prayer upon the Son, while He
  Blesses the dead with His hand silently
To His long day which hours no more offend?

Mother of grace, the pass is difficult,
10 Keen as these rocks, and the bewildered souls
Throng it like echoes, blindly shuddering through.
Thy name, O Lord, each spirit's voice extols,
Whose peace abides in the dark avenue
Amid the bitterness of things occult.

Christina Rossetti

CHRISTINA ROSSETTI was the younger sister of Dante Gabriel. Her Anglican piety links her as a poet with Keble and with seventeenth-century writers like Herbert and Vaughan. Her passionate and romantic nature was disciplined by religious conviction, but any conflict in her personal life emerges in her poetry as the need for obedience and humility. The feeling in her poetry of the ineffable nature of human love, and the impossibility of achieving its fulfilment, save in identity with the will of God, brings her work near to mysticism. Of the two following poems, the first was written in March, 1864, and belongs to a group of poems written during a period when she was experiencing profound depression and a feeling of self-reproach. The date of the other poem is uncertain, but expresses something of the same sense of desolation and a longing for peace in submission to God.

WHO SHALL DELIVER ME?

God strengthen me to bear myself;
That heaviest weight of all to bear,
Inalienable weight of care.

All others are outside myself;
5 I lock my door and bar them out,
The turmoil, tedium, gad-about.

I lock my door upon myself
And bar them out; but who shall wall
Self from myself, most loathed of all?

10 If I could once lay down myself,
And start self-purged upon the race
That all must run! Death runs apace.

If I could set aside myself,
And start with lightened heart upon
15 The road by all men overgone!

God harden me against myself,
This coward with pathetic voice
Who craves for ease, and rest, and joys:

Myself, arch-traitor to myself;
20 My hollowest friend, my deadliest foe,
My clog whatever road I go.

Yet One there is can curb myself,
Can roll the strangling load from me,
Break off the yoke and set me free.

NONE OTHER LAMB, NONE OTHER NAME

None other Lamb, none other Name,
None other Hope in heaven or earth or sea,
None other Hiding-place from guilt and shame,
None beside Thee.

5 My faith burns low, my hope burns low,
Only my heart's desire cries out in me
By the deep thunder of its want and woe,
Cries out to Thee.

Lord, Thou art Life tho' I be dead,
10 Love's Fire Thou art, however cold I be:
Nor heaven have I, nor place to lay my head,
Nor home, but Thee.

Coventry Patmore

'FAINT YET PURSUING'

PATMORE's spiritual pilgrimage was a reversal of the journey undertaken by many of his contemporaries. He was brought up by an agnostic father, but a reading of Coleridge's *Aids to Reflection* led him to Christianity and to membership of the Church of England. Coleridge was a great influence upon him, in poetry, in theology, and in politics. Patmore, indeed, was one of the first to assess justly the part played by Coleridge in forming nineteenth-century opinions. In the first of four essays on Coleridge, which Patmore contributed to the *St. James's Gazette* in 1886–7, he wrote: "To him more than to any other Englishman of the present century, we are indebted for such 'sweetness and light' as our present culture possesses." Patmore's most famous work was *The Angel in the House*, two instalments of which appeared in 1854–6. The writing of this poem, which celebrated conjugal love as a prefiguration of the human-divine encounter, was interrupted by the death of his first wife, Emily, in 1862. After his wife's death, Patmore became a Roman Catholic and remarried in 1864. In 1868 he published a small volume of nine odes, which he added to in two enlarged editions entitled *The Unknown Eros*, 1877–8, and containing "Faint yet pursuing". This poem describes the constant struggle of the religious life, and it has been suggested (by F. Page, *Patmore, A Study in Poetry*, 1933) that in writing it Patmore had in mind the title of Dickens's Christmas Book, *The Battle of Life*. Patmore, in a review of Dickens's story in the *North British Review* for May, 1847, made it clear that he rejected its facile and sentimental optimism and considered man's moral struggle as ". . . . not a battle, but a weary life's campaign". The form of the ode used here by Patmore, with its irregular long and short lines, probably owes something to Wordsworth's *Ode: Intimations of Immortality* and to the choruses of Milton's *Samson Agonistes*. Patmore was keenly interested in questions of metrics, and the published correspondence of Gerard Manley Hopkins provides information of the views of the two men on this subject.

Heroic Good, target for which the young
Dream in their dreams that every bow is strung,
And, missing, sigh
Unfruitful, or as disbelievers die,

The title of the poem is a quotation from *Judges*, viii, 4, which refers to Gideon's pursuit of the Midianites.

5 Thee having miss'd, I will not so revolt,
But lowlier shoot my bolt,
And lowlier still, if still I may not reach,
And my proud stomach teach
That less than highest is good, and may be high.
10 An even walk in life's uneven way,
Though to have dreamt of flight and not to fly
Be strange and sad,
Is not a boon that's given to all who pray.
If this I had
15 I'd envy none!
Nay, trod I straight for one
Year, month or week,
Should Heaven withdraw, and Satan me amerce
Of power and joy, still would I seek
20 Another victory with a like reverse;
Because the good of victory does not die,
As dies the failure's curse,
And what we have to gain
Is, not one battle, but a weary life's campaign.
25 Yet meaner lot being sent
Should more than me content;
Yea, if I lie
Among vile shards, though born for silver wings,
In the strong flight and feathers gold
30 Of whatsoever heavenward mounts and sings
I must by admiration so comply
That there I should my own delight behold.
Yea, though I sin each day times seven,
And dare not lift the fearfullest eyes to Heaven,
35 Thanks must I give
Because that seven times are not eight or nine,
And that my darkness is all mine,
And that I live
Within this oak-shade one more minute even,
40 Hearing the winds their Maker magnify.

18 *amerce:* to exact from.

Algernon Charles Swinburne

HYMN TO PROSERPINE

After the Proclamation in Rome of the Christian Faith

Vicisti, Galilæe

SWINBURNE left Oxford without taking a degree, and as a young man plunged into the bohemian life of London society. He became a friend of Rossetti and was associated with the Pre-Raphaelites. He was a passionate rebel against convention and ardent champion of freedom in thought and behaviour. To many of his contemporaries he seemed a dangerous and Byronic figure who had confused liberty with libertinism. Even those who had abandoned traditional creeds were shocked by his fierce denunciation of Christianity and by the sensuality of his poetry. John Morley, for instance, in a review of *Poems and Ballads* in the *Saturday Review* for August 4, 1866, said that ". . . there is an enormous difference between an attempt to revivify among us the grand old pagan conception of Joy, and an attempt to glorify all the bestial delights that the subtleness of Greek depravity was able to contrive". Swinburne had a great knowledge of classical literature and a profound admiration for ancient Greece, but it was the Greece of pagan naturalism rather than Plato that fired his imagination. His charge against Christianity was that it had destroyed the freshness and vitality of the ancient world and substituted for them a morbid sense of sin. In making this charge, Swinburne undoubtedly chose to shock his contemporaries by attacking Christianity and Christ in terms that the believer would find blasphemous. The *Hymn to Proserpine*, which was published in *Poems and Ballads*, 1866, provides a good illustration of this. Here Swinburne extols the pagan queen of the underworld, Proserpina, and laments the victory of Christ, the "pale Galilean", whose reign has brought a grey drabness to the human spirit. But, declares Swinburne, this reign, too, will disappear and the world will again be liberated:

Yet thy kingdom shall pass, Galilean, thy dead shall
go down to thee dead.

The *Hymn* is put into the mouth of a pagan Roman of the fourth century A.D. The *Proclamation* of the sub-title is Constantine's Edict of Milan (A.D. 313) which gave official recognition to Christianity. *Vicisti, Galilæe* (Thou hast conquered, O Galilean) were supposed to be the last words of the Emperor Julian, who died in A.D. 363, and who had opposed Christianity throughout his life-time.

I have lived long enough, having seen one thing, that love
hath an end;

Goddess and maiden and queen, be near me now and befriend.
Thou art more than the day or the morrow, the seasons that
 laugh or that weep;
For these give joy and sorrow; but thou, Proserpina, sleep.
5 Sweet is the treading of wine, and sweet the feet of the
 dove;
But a goodlier gift is thine than foam of the grapes or love.
Yea, is not even Apollo, with hair and harpstring of gold,
A bitter God to follow, a beautiful God to behold?
I am sick of singing: the bays burn deep and chafe: I am fain
10 To rest a little from praise and grievous pleasure and pain.
For the Gods we know not of, who give us our daily breath,
We know they are cruel as love or life, and lovely as death.
O Gods dethroned and deceased, cast forth, wiped out in a
 day!
From your wrath is the world released, redeemed from your
 chains, men say.
15 New Gods are crowned in the city; their flowers have broken
 your rods;
They are merciful, clothed with pity, the young compassionate
 Gods.
But for me their new device is barren, the days are bare;
Things long past over suffice, and men forgotten that were.
Time and the Gods are at strife; ye dwell in the midst thereof,
20 Draining a little life from the barren breasts of love.
I say to you, cease, take rest; yea, I say to you all, be at
 peace,
Till the bitter milk of her breast and the barren bosom shall
 cease.
Wilt thou yet take all, Galilean? but these thou shalt not take,
The laurel, the palms and the paean, the breasts of the nymphs
 in the brake;
25 Breasts more soft than a dove's, that tremble with tenderer
 breath;

9 *bays:* the laurel leaves which formed the poet's crown.

15 *New Gods:* the Christian saints who would be regarded as gods by a pagan. *rods:* i.e. the symbols of authority and chastisement.

And all the wings of the Loves, and all the joy before death;
All the feet of the hours that sound as a single lyre,
Dropped and deep in the flowers, with strings that flicker like fire.
More than these wilt thou give, things fairer than all these things?
30 Nay, for a little we live, and life hath mutable wings.
A little while and we die; shall life not thrive as it may?
For no man under the sky lives twice, outliving his day.
And grief is a grievous thing, and a man hath enough of his tears:
Why should he labour, and bring fresh grief to blacken his years?
35 Thou hast conquered, O pale Galilean; the world has grown grey from thy breath;
We have drunken of things Lethean, and fed on the fullness of death.
Laurel is green for a season, and love is sweet for a day;
But love grows bitter with treason, and laurel outlives not May.
Sleep, shall we sleep after all? for the world is not sweet in the end;
40 For the old faiths loosen and fall, the new years ruin and rend.
Fate is a sea without shore, and the soul is a rock that abides;
But her ears are vexed with the roar and her face with the foam of the tides.
O lips that the live blood faints in, the leavings of racks and rods!
O ghastly glories of saints, dead limbs of gibbeted Gods!
45 Though all men abase them before you in spirit, and all knees bend,
I kneel not neither adore you, but standing, look to the end.

27 *hours:* The Horæ in classical mythology were the goddesses of the seasons.

36 *Lethean:* Lethe was the River of Forgetfulness in the classical underworld.

All delicate days and pleasant, all spirits and sorrows are cast
Far out with the foam of the present that sweeps to the surf of the past:
Where beyond the extreme sea-wall, and between the remote sea-gates,
50 Waste water washes, and tall ships founder, and deep death waits:
Where, mighty with deepening sides, clad about with the seas as with wings,
And impelled of invisible tides, and fulfilled of unspeakable things,
White-eyed and poisonous-finned, shark-toothed and serpentine-curled,
Rolls, under the whitening wind of the future, the wave of the world.
55 The depths stand naked in sunder behind it, the storms flee away;
In the hollow before it the thunder is taken and snared as a prey;
In its sides is the north-wind bound; and its salt is of all men's tears;
With light of ruin, and sound of changes, and pulse of years:
With travail of day after day, and with trouble of hour upon hour;
60 And bitter as blood is the spray; and the crests are as fangs that devour:
And its vapour and storm of its steam as the sighing of spirits to be;
And its noise as the noise in a dream; and its depth as the roots of the sea:
And the height of its heads as the height of the utmost stars of the air:
And the ends of the earth at the might thereof tremble, and time is made bare.
65 Will ye bridle the deep sea with reins, will ye chasten the high sea with rods?
Will ye take her to chain her with chains, who is older than all ye Gods?

All ye as a wind shall go by, as a fire shall ye pass and be past;
Ye are Gods, and behold, ye shall die, and the waves be upon you at last.
In the darkness of time, in the deeps of the years, in the changes of things,
70 Ye shall sleep as a slain man sleeps, and the world shall forget you for kings.
Though the feet of thine high priests tread where thy lords and our forefathers trod,
Though these that were Gods are dead, and thou being dead art a God,
Though before thee the throned Cytherean be fallen, and hidden her head,
Yet thy kingdom shall pass, Galilean, thy dead shall go down to thee dead.
75 Of the maiden thy mother men sing as a goddess with grace clad around;
Thou art throned where another was king; where another was queen she is crowned.
Yea, once we had sight of another: but now she is queen, say these.
Not as thine, not as thine was our mother, a blossom of flowering seas,
Clothed round with the world's desire as with raiment, and fair as the foam,
80 And fleeter than kindled fire, and a goddess, and mother of Rome.
For thine came pale and a maiden, and sister to sorrow; but ours,
Her deep hair heavily laden with odour and colour of flowers,
White rose of the rose-white water, a silver splendour, a flame,
Bent down unto us that besought her, and earth grew sweet with her name.

73 *Cytherean:* Aphrodite, or Venus, was said to have been born out of the waves at Cythera.

80 *mother of Rome:* Aeneas, the mythical founder of Rome, was said to have been the son of Aphrodite.

85 For thine came weeping, a slave among slaves, and rejected; but she
Came flushed from the full-flushed wave, and imperial, her foot on the sea.
And the wonderful waters knew her, the winds and the viewless ways,
And the roses grew rosier, and bluer the sea-blue stream of the bays.
Ye are fallen, our lords, by what token? we wist that ye should not fall.
90 Ye were all so fair that are broken; and one more fair than ye all.
But I turn to her still, having seen she shall surely abide in the end;
Goddess and maiden and queen, be near me now and befriend.
O daughter of earth, of my mother, her crown and blossom of birth,
I am also, I also, thy brother; I go as I came unto earth.
95 In the night where thine eyes are as moons are in heaven, the night where thou art,
Where the silence is more than all tunes, where sleep overflows from the heart,
Where the poppies are sweet as the rose in our world, and the red rose is white,
And the wind falls faint as it blows with the fume of the flowers of the night,
And the murmur of spirits that sleep in the shadow of Gods from afar
100 Grows dim in thine ears and deep as the deep dim soul of a star,
In the sweet low light of thy face, under heavens untrod by the sun,
Let my soul with their souls find place, and forget what is done and undone.
Thou art more than the Gods who number the days of our temporal breath;

97 *poppies:* The poppy, the sacred flower of Proserpina, is used in the production of opium and is therefore the flower of oblivion.

For these give labour and slumber; but thou, Proserpina, death.
105 Therefore now at thy feet I abide for a season in silence. I know
I shall die as my fathers died, and sleep as they sleep; even so.
For the glass of the years is brittle wherein we gaze for a span;
A little soul for a little bears up this corpse which is man.
So long I endure, no longer; and laugh not again, neither weep.
110 For there is no God found stronger than death; and death is a sleep.

George Meredith

MODERN LOVE

IN 1849 Meredith married Mary Nicolls, the widowed daughter of the novelist, Thomas Love Peacock. His wife was a beautiful and intelligent woman, but very neurotic, and the marriage ended disastrously in 1858, when Mrs. Meredith left her husband for another man. This union, too, was a failure and Meredith's wife died in 1861, a miserable and tormented figure. In the following year Meredith published *Modern Love*. This cycle of poems must not be taken as a factual record of the poet's own marriage, but there can be no doubt that his unhappy experience finds release here. There are fifty poems in the cycle and each of them has sixteen lines divided into four quatrains. The title *Modern Love* has a twofold reference. Firstly, there is irony in the adjective *modern*, for however enlightened these modern lovers may be, they find that knowledge alone gives no solution to their difficulties. Secondly, Meredith breaks new ground in these poems. The complete cycle records not the external events of this disintegrating marriage, but the inner conflicts, the psychological incompatibility, the strange and shifting balance of love and hate that relate the two main characters. Meredith comes very close to the modern novel in these poems. He never had religious faith, and, unlike so many of his contemporaries, did not experience the struggle of abandoning or defending his beliefs. For him, Nature takes the place of God, and he believed that man could achieve peace of mind and moral certitude by accepting his place in the natural process. In the following two poems from *Modern Love* this belief is expressed not optimistically, but with a recognition that the individual life still remains a tragic mystery.

XIII

"I play for Seasons; not Eternities!"
Says Nature, laughing on her way. "So must
All those whose stake is nothing more than dust!"
And lo, she wins, and of her harmonies
5 She is full sure! Upon her dying rose
She drops a look of fondness, and goes by,
Scarce any retrospection in her eye;
For she the laws of growth most deeply knows,
Whose hands bear, here, a seed-bag—there, an urn.
10 Pledged she herself to aught, 'twould mark her end!
This lesson of our only visible friend
Can we not teach our foolish hearts to learn?
Yes! yes!—but, oh, our human rose is fair
Surpassingly! Lose calmly Love's great bliss,
15 When the renewed for ever of a kiss
Whirls life within the shower of loosened hair!

L

Thus piteously Love closed what he begat:
The union of this ever-diverse pair!
These two were rapid falcons in a snare,
Condemned to do the flitting of the bat.
5 Lovers beneath the singing sky of May,
They wandered once; clear as the dew on flowers:
But they fed not on the advancing hours:
Their hearts held cravings for the buried day.

11 *visible friend:* i.e. Nature.

13 *human rose:* i.e. human love, which perishes like the other roses.

15-16 The kiss and physical contact seem to promise eternal love. How difficult it is to accept love as merely transitory.

3-4 The image of the lovers as "falcons in a snare" suggests that they have lost their freedom in marriage. The image of the bat suggests that they have been reduced to aimlessness and blindness.

Then each applied to each that fatal knife,
10 Deep questioning, which probes to endless dole.
Ah, what a dusty answer gets the soul
When hot for certainties in this our life!—
In tragic hints here see what evermore
Moves dark as yonder midnight ocean's force,
15 Thundering like ramping hosts of warrior horse,
To throw that faint thin line upon the shore!

16 In the closing lines human feelings are compared to the movement of the ocean which, for all its power, leaves only a faint line of foam upon the shore.

James Thomson

from
THE CITY OF DREADFUL NIGHT

JAMES THOMSON (who sometimes wrote under the *nom-de-plume* of B.V. or "Bysshe Vanolis") began writing *The City of Dreadful Night* in 1870, but it was not published until 1874, when it appeared by instalments in the *National Reformer*. Thomson, for much of his life, struggled against ill-health, poverty, and a constitutional melancholy which finally drove him into alcoholism. Several of his poems are written in a happier mood, but *The City of Dreadful Night* is the poem by which he will always be remembered. Writing to his sister-in-law, Thomson described his poem as "sombre and atheistical". Thomson knew Dante's work well and his poem is a kind of *Inferno*, in which London at night becomes a nightmare version of Hell. *The City of Dreadful Night* traverses the whole range of human despair and is entirely without hope; all that one is left with in the final section (which is reprinted here) is the consolation of stoic defiance. Thomson sent the numbers of the *National Reformer* which contained the poem to George Eliot, who replied that she wished he had used "more heroic strains with a wider embrace of human fellowship in them". Thomson's poem is not a philosophical defence of atheism, but a vision of black despair which springs from a deep depression of the spirit. Its author realised something of its subjective character when he wrote: "I am aware that the truth of midnight does not exclude the truth of noonday, though one's nature may lead him to dwell in the former rather than the latter."

Anear the centre of that northern crest
  Stands out a level upland bleak and bare,
From which the city east and south and west
  Sinks gently in long waves; and thronèd there
5 An Image sits, stupendous, superhuman,
The bronze colossus of a wingèd Woman,
  Upon a graded granite base foursquare.

Low-seated she leans forward massively,
  With cheek on clenched left hand, the forearm's might
10 Erect, its elbow on her rounded knee;
  Across a clasped book in her lap the right
Upholds a pair of compasses; she gazes
With full set eyes, but wandering in thick mazes
  Of sombre thought beholds no outward sight.

15 Words cannot picture her; but all men know
  That solemn sketch the pure sad artist wrought
Three centuries and threescore years ago,
  With phantasies of his peculiar thought:
The instruments of carpentry and science
20 Scattered about her feet, in strange alliance
  With the keen wolf-hound sleeping undistraught;

Scales, hour-glass, bell, and magic-square above;
  The grave and solid infant perched beside,
With open winglets that might bear a dove,

6 *Woman:* The Woman, as the poem proceeds to make clear, is Melancholy. Thomson possessed a copy of Albrecht Dürer's *Melencolia* (a copper plate engraving of 1514) and wrote a separate short poem about it. The symbolism used by Thomson in these stanzas is taken from Dürer's picture.

16 *artist:* i.e. Albrecht Dürer (1471–1528).

21 *wolf-hound:* In a letter to William Rossetti, Thomson wrote that he had thought the animal was a dead sheep, awaiting dissection, but that Ruskin believed it to be a sleeping wolf-hound.

22 *Scales,* etc.: A great deal has been written about the symbols used by Dürer and adopted by Thomson in this and the following stanzas. For a detailed commentary, the reader is advised to consult Wilhelm Waetzoldt's *Dürer*, Phaidon Press, 1955, pp. 76–83.

25 Intent upon its tablets, heavy-eyed;
Her folded wings as of a mighty eagle,
But all too impotent to lift the regal
Robustness of her earth-born strength and pride;

And with those wings, and that light wreath which seems
30 To mock her grand head and the knotted frown
Of forehead charged with baleful thoughts and dreams,
The household bunch of keys, the housewife's gown
Voluminous, indented, and yet rigid
As if a shell of burnished metal frigid,
35 The feet thick-shod to tread all weakness down;

The comet hanging o'er the waste dark seas,
The massy rainbow curved in front of it
Beyond the village with the masts and trees;
The snaky imp, dog-headed, from the Pit,
40 Bearing upon its batlike leathern pinions
Her name unfolded in the sun's dominions,
The "MELENCOLIA" that transcends all wit.

Thus has the artist copied her, and thus
Surrounded to expound her form sublime,
45 Her fate heroic and calamitous;
Fronting the dreadful mysteries of Time,
Unvanquished in defeat and desolation,
Undaunted in the hopeless conflagration
Of the day setting on her baffled prime.

50 Baffled and beaten back she works on still,
Weary and sick of soul she works the more,
Sustained by her indomitable will:
The hands shall fashion and the brain shall pore,
And all her sorrow shall be turned to labour,
55 Till Death the friend-foe piercing with his sabre
That mighty heart of hearts ends bitter war.

25 *tablets:* i.e. writing tablets, or perhaps books of wisdom.

But as if blacker night could dawn on night,
  With tenfold gloom on moonless night unstarred,
A sense more tragic than defeat and blight,
60 More desperate than strife with hope debarred,
More fatal than the adamantine Never
Encompassing her passionate endeavour,
  Dawns glooming in her tenebrous regard:

The sense that every struggle brings defeat
65 Because Fate holds no prize to crown success;
That all the oracles are dumb or cheat
  Because they have no secret to express;
That none can pierce the vast black veil uncertain
Because there is no light beyond the curtain;
70 That all is vanity and nothingness.

Titanic from her high throne in the north,
  That City's sombre Patroness and Queen,
In bronze sublimity she gazes forth
  Over her Capital of teen and threne,
75 Over the river with its isles and bridges,
The marsh and moorland, to the stern rock-ridges,
  Confronting them with a coëval mien.

The moving moon and stars from east to west
  Circle before her in the sea of air;
80 Shadows and gleams glide round her solemn rest.
  Her subjects often gaze up to her there:
The strong to drink new strength of iron endurance,
The weak new terrors; all, renewed assurance
  And confirmation of the old despair.

74 *teen and threne:* archaic words meaning "trouble" and "lamentation".

77 *coëval mien:* a look of equal age; i.e. Melancholy is as old as Nature herself.

Gerard Manley Hopkins

THE WRECK OF THE DEUTSCHLAND

G. M. HOPKINS went up to Balliol College, Oxford, in 1863. His reading of Newman's *Apologia pro Vita Sua* in 1864 and his subsequent correspondence with Newman led the way to his conversion to the Roman Catholic faith in 1866. He joined the Society of Jesus, and after ordination worked as a priest in the slums of Liverpool and as Professor of Greek in the recently established Catholic University of Dublin. His religious profession resulted in strained relations between Hopkins and his family and between Hopkins's poetic aspirations and his religious obedience. On becoming a Jesuit Hopkins burned most of his early poetry and "resolved to write no more . . . unless it were by the wish of my superiors". His poetry was not published in fact until 1918. His major poem, *The Wreck of the Deutschland*, was written with the encouragement of his rector on the occasion of the death by drowning in 1875 of five Franciscan nuns, who were exiled from Germany because of their religious beliefs. In a letter to his friend Canon Dixon, Hopkins wrote, "I had long had haunting my ear the echo of a new rhythm which now I realised on paper". This rhythm was what Hopkins called "sprung rhythm", a metrical form that depends on the number of stresses in a line rather than the number of syllables, and which has affinities with the alliterative measures of medieval poetry. Hopkins's poetry indeed is not typically Victorian in form or content. If he returns for inspiration to earlier verse forms, so his thought was influenced by the medieval philosopher, Duns Scotus, and by the founder of his Order, Ignatius Loyola. But his poetry, both in form and content, bears the stamp of a highly individual and brilliant personality. *The Wreck of the Deutschland*, in the true elegiac tradition, attempts to justify divine providence. The poem is in four parts. Hopkins begins with a meditation on the paradox that God's judgment or wrath is at one with his mercy. This introductory part proceeds to reflect upon God's dealing with the individual, and ends with the poet's prayer that God will master his rebellious self either by some sudden crisis or by a gradual submission of the poet's will. Stanzas 11-17 describe the wreck itself. The third part, stanzas 18-31, centres on the figure of the heroic nun, who takes upon herself the self-sacrificial nature of Christ. The last part expresses the poet's acceptance of the divine will for himself, and ends with a prayer for the "stirring of English souls" towards God.

To the
happy memory of five Franciscan Nuns
*exiles by the Falk Laws**
drowned between midnight and morning of
Dec. 7th, 1875

PART THE FIRST

1

Thou mastering me
God! giver of breath and bread;
World's strand, sway of the sea;
Lord of living and dead;
5 Thou hast bound bones and veins in me, fastened me flesh,
And after it almost unmade, what with dread,
Thy doing: and dost thou touch me afresh?
Over again I feel thy finger and find thee.

2

I did say yes
10 O at lightning and lashed rod;
Thou heardst me truer than tongue confess
Thy terror, O Christ, O God;
Thou knowest the walls, altar and hour and night:
The swoon of a heart that the sweep and the hurl of thee trod
15 Hard down with a horror of height:
And the midriff astrain with leaning of, laced with fire of stress.

* The Falk Laws were so called after Dr. Falk (1827-1900), the Prussian Minister of Education under Bismarck. They were laws which subjected the Roman Catholic Church in Germany to control by the state.

16 *stress:* a word to which Hopkins gave especial significance. "Stress" (or "instress") for Hopkins meant the perception of "inscape", and "inscape" was the particular and unique quality of every event and object, its quintessence. Here the word refers especially to the unique and sometimes terrifying experience of falling into the hands of God.

3

The frown of his face
Before me, the hurtle of hell
Behind, where, where was a, where was a place?
20 I whirled out wings that spell
And fled with a fling of the heart to the heart of the Host.
My heart, but you were dovewinged, I can tell,
Carrier-witted, I am bold to boast,
To flash from the flame to the flame then, tower from the grace to the grace.

4

25 I am soft sift
In an hourglass—at the wall
Fast, but mined with a motion, a drift,
And it crowds and it combs to the fall;
I steady as a water in a well, to a poise, to a pane,
30 But roped with, always, all the way down from the tall
Fells or flanks of the voel, a vein
Of the gospel proffer, a pressure, a principle, Christ's gift.

20 *that spell:* "spell" is a noun here; hence the phrase means "in that short period of time".

23 *Carrier-witted:* the heart has been compared to a dove, now it is like a homing pigeon.

27 *mined:* undermined.

28 *combs:* i.e. falls away into valleys or combs.

29 *pane:* a lock in an irrigation system that keeps the water from running away. The image in 29-32 is of a head of water kept at constant level by pressure from the springs that feed into it. God's grace is an outside pressure that sustains a man's spiritual strength. The springs of water that run down the mountain side look like ropes, constantly running but with the appearance of immobility.

31 *voel:* a bare hillside or watershed (Welsh *y foel*). Hopkins wrote the poem while he was in Wales.

32 *proffer:* Here the word is a noun meaning something proffered.

5

I kiss my hand
To the stars, lovely-asunder
35 Starlight, wafting him out of it; and
Glow, glory in thunder;
Kiss my hand to the dappled-with-damson west:
Since, tho' he is under the world's splendour and wonder,
His mystery must be instressed, stressed;
40 For I greet him the days I meet him, and bless when I understand.

6

Not out of his bliss
Springs the stress felt
Nor first from heaven (and few know this)
Swings the stroke dealt—
45 Stroke and a stress that stars and storms deliver,
That guilt is hushed by, hearts are flushed by and melt—
But it rides time like riding a river
(And here the faithful waver, the faithless fable and miss).

7

It dates from day
50 Of his going in Galilee;

39 *instressed, stressed:* See note on line 16. The meaning of this and the preceding line is that although God is perceived in the beauty of Nature, we really meet him in ourselves, in the unique context of our own inner consciousness.

41–8 The meaning of this stanza is that we are closest to God not in moments of spiritual joy but in adversity and suffering, though the latter are not "sent" by God (*Nor first from heaven . . . Swings the stroke dealt*) but are part of the natural order (*a stress that stars and storms deliver*). This stress of God's dealing with us hushes our guilt and cleanses and melts the rebellious human heart.

47 *it:* i.e. the stress. The suffering that comes to us as part of the natural order is not "sent" by God, but it is used by God. Its purpose is a mystery which cannot be apprehended in time, but will become clear outside and beyond time.

Warm-laid grave of a womb-life grey;
Manger, maiden's knee;
The dense and the driven Passion, and frightful sweat;
Thence the discharge of it, there its swelling to be,
55 Though felt before, though in high flood yet—
What none would have known of it, only the heart, being hard at bay,

8

Is out with it! Oh,
We lash with the best or worst
Word last! How a lush-kept plush-capped sloe
60 Will, mouthed to flesh-burst,
Gush!—flush the man, the being with it, sour or sweet,
Brim, in a flash, full!—Hither then, last or first,
To hero of Calvary, Christ's feet—
Never ask if meaning it, wanting it, warned of it—men go.

9

65 Be adored among men,
God, three-numberèd form;
Wring thy rebel, dogged in den,
Man's malice, with wrecking and storm.
Beyond saying sweet, past telling of tongue,
70 Thou art lightning and love, I found it, a winter and warm;
Father and fondler of heart thou hast wrung:
Hast thy dark descending and most art merciful then.

56 *hard at bay:* It is when suffering becomes acute and the heart is "hard at bay" that we recognise the significance of Christ's Passion, and realise that God suffered and is still suffering with us.

61 *sour or sweet:* Christian experience is a mixture of sorrow and joy, and Hopkins uses the eating of a sloe as an image of this bitter-sweet quality.

66 *three-numberèd:* a reference to the Trinity, three persons and one God. The stanza develops the thought (crystallised in the phrase, *Thou art lightning and love*) that God's wrath is an instrument of his mercy. God will overcome man's rebelliousness, obstinacy and malice, with suffering.

10

With an anvil-ding
And with fire in him forge thy will
75 Or rather, rather then, stealing as Spring
Through him, melt him but master him still:
Whether at once, as once at a crash Paul,
Or as Austin, a lingering-out sweet skill,
Make mercy in all of us, out of us all
80 Mastery, but be adored, but be adored King.

PART THE SECOND

11

"Some find me a sword; some
The flange and the rail; flame,
Fang, or flood" goes Death on drum,
And storms bugle his fame.
85 But wé dream we are rooted in earth—Dust!
Flesh falls within sight of us, we, though our flower the same,
Wave with the meadow, forget that there must
The sour scythe cringe, and the blear share come.

12

On Saturday sailed from Bremen,
90 American-outward-bound,

77 *Paul:* The contrast here is between the conversion of St. Paul which was sudden and dramatic (*Acts*, ix) and that of St. Augustine (Austin) which took several years (*Confessions of St. Augustine*).

81-4 In this and the following lines Death is personified as a recruiting sergeant calling men to his colours. Men meet death in various ways: in battle (*a sword*); at the end of life's journey (*The flange and the rail* lead the traveller to the railway terminus); or by accident (*flame, Fang, or flood*).

88 *sour:* The adjective refers back to line 61. The verb *cringe* is transitive and suggests the bending over and cutting of the grass. The adjective *blear* suggests both our own indistinct apprehension of death and its indiscriminate (because half-blinded) action.

Take settler and seamen, tell men with women,
Two hundred souls in the round—
O Father, not under thy feathers nor ever as guessing
The goal was a shoal, of a fourth the doom to be drowned;
95 Yet did the dark side of the bay of thy blessing
Not vault them, the millions of rounds of thy mercy not reeve even them in?

13

Into the snows she sweeps,
Hurling the haven behind,
The Deutschland, on Sunday; and so the sky keeps,
100 For the infinite air is unkind,
And the sea flint-flake, black-backed in the regular blow,
Sitting Eastnortheast, in cursed quarter, the wind;
Wiry and white-fiery and whirlwind-swivellèd snow
Spins to the widow-making unchilding unfathering deeps.

14

105 She drove in the dark to leeward,
She struck—not a reef or a rock
But the combs of a smother of sand: night drew her
Dead to the Kentish Knock;
And she beat the bank down with her bows and the ride of her keel:
110 The breakers rolled on her beam with ruinous shock;
And canvas and compass, the whorl and the wheel
Idle for ever to waft her or wind her with, these she endured.

91 *tell:* count.
96 *reeve:* a nautical term meaning to make fast with a rope.
rounds: the turns in the rope.
107 *combs:* depressions or valleys in the sandbank.
108 *Kentish Knock:* a sandbank near the Thames estuary.
111 *whorl:* a fly-wheel; presumably it means here part of the steering gear.
112 *wind:* steer.

15

Hope had grown grey hairs,
Hope had mourning on,
115 Trenched with tears, carved with cares,
Hope was twelve hours gone;
And frightful a nightfall folded rueful a day
Nor rescue, only rocket and lightship, shone,
And lives at last were washing away:
120 To the shrouds they took,—they shook in the hurling and horrible airs.

16

One stirred from the rigging to save
The wild woman-kind below,
With a rope's end round the man, handy and brave—
He was pitched to his death at a blow,
125 For all his dreadnought breast and braids of thew:
They could tell him for hours, dandled the to and fro
Through the cobbled foam-fleece, what could he do
With the burl of the fountains of air, buck and the flood of the wave?

17

They fought with God's cold—
130 And they could not and fell to the deck
(Crushed them) or water (and drowned them) or rolled
With the sea-romp over the wreck.
Night roared, with the heart-break hearing a heart-broke rabble,

125 *thew:* muscle.

126 *tell . . . dandled:* They could count his swinging movements.

127 *cobbled:* covered with patches, with the appearance of cobblestones.

128 *burl:* literally means lump. *buck:* This is an archaic word with several meanings. Two of them are appropriate here: "rearing" or "drenching".

The woman's wailing, the crying of child without check—
135 Till a lioness arose breasting the babble,
A prophetess towered in the tumult, a virginal tongue told.

18

Ah, touched in your bower of bone
Are you! turned for an exquisite smart,
Have you! make words break from me here all alone,
140 Do you!—mother of being in me, heart.
O unteachably after evil, but uttering truth,
Why, tears! is it? tears; such a melting, a madrigal start!
Never-eldering revel and river of youth,
What can it be, this glee? the good you have there of your own?

19

145 Sister, a sister calling
A master, her master and mine!—
And the inboard seas run swirling and hawling;
The rash smart sloggering brine
Blinds her; but she that weather sees one thing, one;
150 Has one fetch in her: she rears herself to divine
Ears, and the call of the tall nun
To the men in the tops and the tackle rode over the storm's brawling.

20

She was first of a five and came
Of a coifèd sisterhood.

141 *after:* i.e. in pursuit of.

142 *madrigal:* In this stanza the poet records the effect of the nun's words upon him. His tears and grief are wiped away by her heroism, and his poem becomes not a dirge but a *madrigal* (i.e. a lyric outpouring) and a *glee* (i.e. a song of happiness).

147 *hawling:* i.e. running or being pulled back.

150 *fetch:* i.e. purpose or course.

154 *coifèd:* A coif is a close-fitting cap, and the word refers to the nuns' habit.

155 (O Deutschland, double a desperate name!
O world wide of its good!
But Gertrude, lily, and Luther, are two of a town,
Christ's lily and beast of the waste wood:
From life's dawn it is drawn down,
160 Abel is Cain's brother and breasts they have sucked the same.)

21

Loathed for a love men knew in them,
Banned by the land of their birth,
Rhine refused them. Thames would ruin them;
Surf, snow, river and earth
165 Gnashed: but thou art above, thou Orion of light;
Thy unchancelling poising palms were weighing the worth,
Thou martyr-master: in thy sight
Storm flakes were scroll-leaved flowers, lily showers—sweet heaven was astrew in them.

22

Five! the finding and sake
170 And cipher of suffering Christ.
Mark, the mark is of man's make
And the word of it Sacrificed.

155 *Deutschland . . . desperate:* A doubly desperate name, because it is the name of the vessel and of the country which exiled them.

157 *Gertrude . . . Luther:* St. Gertrude lived at Eisleben in the 13th century, and later this was the birthplace of Martin Luther.

165 *Orion:* The constellation Orion figures the Greek giant as a hunter. The poet sees God as a hunter, pursuing the nuns with ruthless love.

169 *Five:* In this stanza the poet uses the number *five* as a conceit. There were five nuns, just as the wounds (the *stigmata*) on Christ's body were five. The word *Stigma* can mean "branding" as well as "wound", and so the poet uses the number to suggest that the nuns bear this *finding* or *sake* as a mark of their ownership, as sheep are marked by their shepherd. Christ as well as being a shepherd was also the Lamb of God, who bore the mark himself.

But he scores it in scarlet himself on his own bespoken,
Before-time-taken, dearest prizèd and priced—
175 Stigma, signal, cinquefoil token
For lettering of the lamb's fleece, ruddying of the rose-flake.

23

Joy fall to thee, father Francis,
Drawn to the Life that died;
With the gnarls of the nails in thee, niche of the lance, his
180 Lovescape crucified
And seal of his seraph-arrival! and these thy daughters
And five-livèd and leavèd favour and pride,
Are sisterly sealed in wild waters,
To bathe in his fall-gold mercies, to breathe in his all-fire glances.

24

185 Away in the loveable west,
On a pastoral forehead of Wales,
I was under a roof here, I was at rest,
And they the prey of the gales;
She to the black-about air, to the breaker, the thickly
190 Falling flakes, to the throng that catches and quails
Was calling "O Christ, Christ, come quickly":
The cross to her she calls Christ to her, christens her wild-worst Best.

175 *Cinquefoil:* five-leaved.

177 *Francis:* St. Francis of Assissi was reputed to have borne the marks of Christ's *stigmata* on his body. The five nuns belonged to the Franciscan order.

180 *Lovescape:* A running together of "love" and "inscape" (see note on l. 16). It refers to St. Francis's apprehension of Christ's love, an apprehension so intense that it produced the marks of the *stigmata*.

186 *Wales:* Hopkins was at St. Beuno's College in the Vale of Clwyd.

192 *cross . . . Christ:* The verb *calls* has a double object to signify that when Christ comes to the nun it will be as a cross.

25

The majesty! what did she mean?
Breathe, arch and original Breath.
195 Is it love in her of the being as her lover had been?
Breathe, body of lovely Death.
They were else-minded then, altogether, the men
Woke thee with a *we are perishing* in the weather of Gennesareth.
Or is it that she cried for the crown then,
200 The keener to come at the comfort for feeling the combating keen?

26

For how to the heart's cheering
The down-dugged ground-hugged grey
Hovers off, the jay-blue heavens appearing
Of pied and peeled May!
205 Blue-beating and hoary-glow height; or night, still higher,
With belled fire and the moth-soft Milky Way,
What by your measure is the heaven of desire,
The treasure never eyesight got, nor was ever guessed what for the hearing?

27

No, but it was not these.
210 The jading and jar of the cart,

194 *arch . . . Breath:* i.e. the supreme (*arch*) Spirit (*Breath*) which moved upon the face of the waters at the Creation (*Genesis*, i, 2). The line is an invocation to the Holy Spirit.

195 *lover:* i.e. Christ.

198 *Gennesareth:* the Sea of Galilee, where Christ stilled the storm (*Matthew*, xiv).

199 *crown:* the crown of thorns or of martyrdom.

204 *pied and peeled:* i.e. parti-coloured and fresh (as of something just peeled).

208 Cf. "Eye hath not seen, nor ear heard . . . the things which God hath prepared for them that love him." (*I Corinthians*, ii, 9.)

Time's tasking, it is fathers that asking for ease
Of the sodden-with-its-sorrowing heart,
Not danger, electrical horror; then further it finds
The appealing of the Passion is tenderer in prayer apart:
215 Other, I gather, in measure her mind's
Burden, in wind's burly and beat of endragonèd seas.

28

But how shall I . . . make me room there:
Reach me a . . . Fancy, come faster—
Strike you the sight of it? look at it loom there,
220 Thing that she . . . there then! the Master,
Ipse, the only one, Christ, King, Head:
He was to cure the extremity where he had cast her;
Do, deal, lord it with living and dead;
Let him ride, her pride, in his triumph, despatch and have done with his doom there.

29

225 Ah! there was a heart right!
There was single eye!
Read the unshapeable shock night
And knew the who and the why;
Wording it how but by him that present and past,
230 Heaven and earth are word of, worded by?—
The Simon Peter of a soul! to the blast
Tarpeian-fast, but a blown beacon of light.

211 *fathers:* a verb. The meaning of these lines is that it is not disaster, but the quiet tenor of ordinary life that makes us wish for ease. But the appeal of the Passion is most easily met in quiet contemplation, which is something beyond this. Such peace is denied the nun.

225 The heroic nun is the one who sees the religious meaning of the shipwreck.

231 *Simon Peter:* In St. Matthew's account of the storm (Ch. XIV) it was St. Peter who recognised Christ as the figure walking on the waters.

232 *Tarpeian-fast:* a reference to the Tarpeian rock on the Capitoline Hill at Rome. *Peter* means literally "a rock", and St. Peter was first Bishop of Rome.

30

Jesu, heart's light,
Jesu, maid's son,
235 What was the feast followed the night
Thou hadst glory of this nun?—
Feast of the one woman without stain.
For so conceivèd, so to conceive thee is done;
But here was heart-throe, birth of a brain,
240 Word, that heard and kept thee and uttered thee outright.

31

Well, she has thee for the pain, for the
Patience; but pity of the rest of them!
Heart go and bleed at a bitterer vein for the
Comfortless unconfessed of them—
245 No not uncomforted: lovely-felicitous Providence
Finger of a tender of, O of a feathery delicacy, the breast of the
Maiden could obey so, be a bell to, ring of it, and
Startle the poor sheep back! is the shipwrack then a harvest, does tempest carry the grain for thee?

32

I admire thee, master of the tides,
250 Of the Yore-flood, of the year's fall;
The recurb and the recovery of the gulf's sides,
The girth of it and the wharf of it and the wall;
Stanching, quenching ocean of a motionable mind;
Ground of being, and granite of it: past all
255 Grasp God, throned behind
Death with a sovereignty that heeds but hides, bodes but abides;

237 The day of the wreck (December 8) was also the Feast of the Immaculate Conception of the Virgin Mary.

250 *Yore-flood: Yore* means "ancient", and hence the phrase refers to Noah's Flood and, perhaps, to the waters which covered the earth at the Creation. The following lines compare mankind with the ocean, ever moving and yet contained within the shores of God's providence.

33

With a mercy that outrides
The all of water, an ark
For the listener; for the lingerer with a love glides
260 Lower than death and the dark;
A vein for the visiting of the past-prayer, pent in prison,
The-last-breath penitent spirits—the uttermost mark
Our passion-plungèd giant risen,
The Christ of the Father compassionate, fetched in the storm of his strides.

34

265 Now burn, new born to the world,
Doubled-naturèd name,
The heaven-flung, heart-fleshed, maiden-furled
Miracle-in-Mary-of-flame,
Mid-numbered He in three of the thunder-throne!
270 Not a dooms-day dazzle in his coming nor dark as he came;
Kind, but royally reclaiming his own;
A released shower, let flash to the shire, not a lightning of fire hard-hurled.

35

Dame, at our door
Drowned, and among our shoals
275 Remember us in the roads, the heaven-haven of the Reward:

261 *vein:* Cf. l. 31. Here the word probably means a channel for God's grace.

263 *giant:* This refers to Christ in the next line. The whole of this stanza is one sentence of which *Christ* is the subject and *fetched* the verb. Christ in his mercy bestrides the storm to the *uttermost mark* to save the souls of men.

266 *Double-naturèd:* i.e. both God and man.

269 *Mid-numbered:* i.e. the middle name of the Holy Trinity.

275 *roads:* the approaches to a harbour.

Our King back, oh, upon English souls!
Let him easter in us, be a dayspring to the dimness of us, be a crimson-cresseted east,
More brightening her, rare-dear Britain, as his reign rolls,
Pride, rose, prince, hero of us, high-priest,
280 Our hearts' charity's hearth's fire, our thoughts' chivalry's throng's Lord.

280 *our thoughts' . . . Lord:* i.e. the Lord of the kindly thoughts that may crowd or throng our minds.

CARRION COMFORT

HOPKINS died at the comparatively early age of forty-five. His last years were darkened by attacks of depression so severe as to be pathological, and which, as he wrote in a letter, "though they do not affect my judgment, resemble madness". The poems he wrote at this time—the "terrible sonnets", as they are called—reflect the conflict both mental and spiritual of his fine and sensitive personality. They portray a spirit in agony, and yet one never finally defeated or broken in its religious faith. The following sonnet is one of this group and was probably composed in 1885. The title was suggested by Hopkins's friend, Robert Bridges, and, as the first line makes clear, refers to despair. The poem describes a night spent in sleeplessness and troubled dreams. Hopkins in writing the sonnet must have had in mind the story of Jacob who wrestled with God all night at a time of trial and crisis (*Genesis*, xxxii).

Not, I'll not, carrion comfort, Despair, not feast on thee;
Not untwist—slack they may be—these last strands of man
In me ór, most weary, cry *I can no more*. I can;
Can something, hope, wish day come, not choose not to be.
5 But ah, but O thou terrible, why wouldst thou rude on me
Thy wring-world right foot rock? lay a lionlimb against me? scan
With darksome devouring eyes my bruisèd bones? and fan,
O in turns of tempest, me heaped there; me frantic to avoid thee and flee?

5 *rude:* used here as a verb and in the archaic sense of acting harshly or violently.

Why? That my chaff might fly; my grain lie, sheer and clear.
10 Nay in all that toil, that coil, since (seems) I kissed the rod,
Hand rather, my heart lo! lapped strength, stole joy, would laugh, chéer.
Cheer whom though? the hero whose heaven-handling flung me, fóot tród
Me? or me that fought him? O which one? is it each one? That night, that year
Of now done darkness I wretch lay wrestling with (my God!) my God.

9 The image here is of the poet's soul being winnowed as chaff is from wheat and gives added meaning to *fan* in line 7. (See *Luke*, xxii, 31.)

10 *coil:* trouble or confusion.

11 *Hand rather:* a reference to Hopkins's ordination. The meaning of *Hand*, and of *rod* in the previous line is that the poet is ready to accept Christian obedience, especially as he is a priest.

13 *That night, that year:* The night has seemed so long that it has been more like a year.

14 *my God:* The first *my God!* is an exclamation of awe at the thought that he has been wrestling with his God. Like Jacob (see introductory note above), the poet has been unaware of the identity of his assailant.

NO WORST, THERE IS NONE

THIS poem belongs to the same group of "terrible sonnets" as "Carrion Comfort," though the exact date of its composition is not known. There are several echoes of Shakespeare's *King Lear* in the poem, and, like Lear, Hopkins is struggling for sanity and peace of mind in the midst of evil and tumult. The poem is not specifically Christian in temper, but is rather an expression of the soul's anguish and a cry for some relief and a measure of endurance.

No worst, there is none. Pitched past pitch of grief,
More pangs will, schooled at forepangs, wilder wring.
Comforter, where, where is your comforting?

3 *Comforter:* i.e. the Holy Spirit.

Mary, mother of us, where is your relief?
5 My cries heave, herds-long; huddle in a main, a chief
Woe, world-sorrow; on an age-old anvil wince and sing—
Then lull, then leave off. Fury had shrieked "No ling-
ering! Let me be fell: force I must be brief".

O the mind, mind has mountains; cliffs of fall
10 Frightful, sheer, no-man-fathomed. Hold them cheap
May who ne'er hung there. Nor does long our small
Durance deal with that steep or deep. Here! creep,
Wretch, under a comfort serves in a whirlwind: all
Life death does end and each day dies with sleep.

5 *herds-long:* The meaning here is that his cries are at first individual and separate as of isolated sheep. They then join together as the combined cry of a herd and become centred upon the one great "woe", the torment of human experience.

6 *sing:* Iron when beaten on an anvil makes a kind of singing noise.

8 *fell:* evil.

12 *Here! creep:* At the storm's height Lear invites the Fool to creep under his cloak for shelter.

14 The last line sounds the same note of tragic resignation as the end of *King Lear*. It may be that the *comfort* of the previous line is the *carrion comfort* which Hopkins rejects in the poem to which he gave that name.

Lionel Johnson

THE DARK ANGEL

A GRAPHIC account of Johnson as a man and a poet can be found in W. B. Yeats's *Autobiographies*. Johnson was of Welsh extraction, but was brought up in England, and because of his conversion to Roman Catholicism developed a romantic interest in Irish culture and politics. He was a pupil of Walter Pater at Oxford and, like his tutor, combined a scholarly interest in the classics with a belief in Art for Art's sake. He opposed the materialist values of Victorian England with a nostalgic vision of a largely idealised Celtic past. Johnson was a spiritual heir of the Pre-Raphaelites, but he anticipated the poets of the "Celtic twilight", such as Yeats, and his work has features that link it to that of G. M. Hopkins. In many of his poems we find the same spiritual struggle we meet in Hopkins's poetry; the same struggle between Christian obedience and a rebellious spirit. The subject of *The Dark Angel* (1893), is not unlike that of Hopkins's "terrible sonnets", but in Hopkins we feel that the poetry expresses a more personal struggle, whereas in Johnson's poem the struggle is less intense and has been subordinated to the desire to produce an aesthetically pleasing work of art. Johnson's romanticism lacks the cutting-edge of Hopkins's acute introspection, and leads to a rather vague and musical use of words that tends to make a reading of his poem an aesthetic experience only, and not a spiritual one.

Dark Angel, with thine aching lust
To rid the world of penitence:
Malicious Angel, who still dost
My soul such subtile violence!

5 Because of thee, no thought, no thing,
Abides for me undesecrate:
Dark Angel, ever on the wing,
Who never reachest me too late!

1 *Dark Angel:* the spirit of evil, doubt and sensuality that tempts the poet to abandon his religious struggle.

When music sounds, then changest thou
10 Its silvery to a sultry fire:
Nor will thine envious heart allow
Delight untortured by desire.

Through thee, the gracious Muses turn
To Furies, O mine Enemy!
15 And all the things of beauty burn
With flames of evil ecstasy.

Because of thee, the land of dreams
Becomes a gathering place of fears:
Until tormented slumber seems
20 One vehemence of useless tears.

When sunlight glows upon the flowers,
Or ripples down the dancing sea:
Thou, with thy troop of passionate powers,
Beleaguerest, bewilderest, me.

25 Within the breath of autumn woods,
Within the winter silences:
Thy venomous spirit stirs and broods,
O Master of impieties!

The ardour of red flame is thine,
30 And thine the steely soul of ice:
Thou poisonest the fair design
Of nature, with unfair device.

Apples of ashes, golden bright;
Waters of bitterness, how sweet!

33 *Apples of ashes:* Josephus, the First Century Jewish historian, refers to the "apples of Sodom" which were lovely to look at but full of ashes. The term is used figuratively for anything disappointing (Cf. *Deuteronomy*, xxxii, 32). The "waters of bitterness" (l.34) refers to the Dead Sea, the waters of which were thought to account for the "apples of ashes".

35 O banquet of a foul delight,
Prepared by thee, dark Paraclete!

Thou art the whisper in the gloom,
The hinting tone, the haunting laugh:
Thou art the adorner of my tomb,
40 The minstrel of mine epitaph.

I fight thee, in the Holy Name!
Yet, what thou dost, is what God saith:
Tempter! should I escape thy flame,
Thou wilt have helped my soul from Death:

45 The second Death, that never dies,
That cannot die, when time is dead:
Live Death, wherein the lost soul cries,
Eternally uncomforted.

Dark Angel, with thine aching lust!
50 Of two defeats, of two despairs:
Less dread, a change to drifting dust,
Than thine eternity of cares.

Do what thou wilt, thou shalt not so,
Dark Angel! triumph over me:
55 Lonely, unto the Lone I go;
Divine, to the Divinity.

36 *Paraclete:* literally means an advocate, but is the title given to the Holy Spirit (*John*, xiv, 16, etc.). Here the poet sees the Dark Angel as a force opposed to the Holy Spirit.

44 *helped my soul:* i.e. by strengthening the soul through temptation and trial.